# ETHIOPIA

## TITLES IN THE MODERN NATIONS OF THE WORLD SERIES INCLUDE:

Austria
Canada
China
Cuba
England
Ethiopia
Germany
Haiti
Jordan
Italy
Mexico
Norway
Russia
Saudi Arabia
Scotland
Somalia
South Korea
Switzerland
Taiwan

# ETHIOPIA

BY LAUREL CORONA

LUCENT BOOKS
P.O. BOX 289011
SAN DIEGO, CA 92198-9011

On cover: Addis Ababa

Library of Congress Cataloging-in-Publication Data

Corona, Laurel, 1949–
    Ethiopia / by Laurel Corona.
        p.   cm. — (Modern nations of the world)
    Includes bibliographical references and index.
    Summary: Discusses the history, geography, climate, government,
culture, people, and modern aspects of Ethiopia.
    ISBN 1-56006-823-X (hard cover)
    1. Ethiopia—Juvenile literature.  [1. Ethiopia.]  I. Title.   II. Series.
DT373 .C65  2001
963—dc21
                                                                    00-009573
                                                                        CIP
                                                                         AC

Copyright © 2001 by Lucent Books, Inc.
P.O. Box 289011, San Diego, CA 92198-9011
Printed in the U.S.A.

# CONTENTS

# INTRODUCTION

## ANCIENT LAND, MODERN CHALLENGES

Many people in the world are familiar with only one image of Ethiopia. They picture in their mind grown men with legs and arms as thin as twigs, with huge knees, and ribs protruding like grates. They see mothers offering shrunken breasts to children too weak to cry or brush the flies from their faces. Staring out from all the pictures are eyes which, as long as strength remains, show their despair, and once strength is gone, show no emotion at all. These are the faces of the thousands of Ethiopians who sit quietly waiting for the slow death that will surely come to them and to those they love.

Ethiopia has clearly fallen on hard times. It is one of the poorest nations on earth. It has suffered over the last decades from famines and political chaos brought on by drought, poor land management, and strife between regions and ethnic groups. Women continue to be treated as second-class citizens, often suffering physical abuse as a result of traditions going back for centuries. Opportunities for poor, rural Ethiopians—the majority of the population—to escape the grinding poverty of their lives remain rare and elusive. Many of the best and the brightest immigrate to the United States and elsewhere, leaving Ethiopia with fewer and fewer people in a position to help steer the country in a positive direction. And even among those who stay, there is little agreement about what that direction should be. Its strategic location between the Middle East and the rest of Africa, and its cultural and historic links to both, make its fate a matter of global interest and concern. Yet most people who are familiar with the region find it difficult to predict its future and even more difficult to determine how best to assist the country in solving its own problems.

## A UNIQUE HERITAGE

Yet the country cannot be summed up by sad photographs of a land laid waste. Ethiopia has one of the richest cultural heritages in the world, and in fact its ancient splendors rivaled those of Rome, Egypt, and Persia. Its relative isolation, both by choice and by geography, allowed it to evolve in a unique manner. It developed its own forms of both Christianity and Judaism and even its own alphabet, which it still uses today. Its ethnic heritage is diverse, having incorporated new arrivals over the centuries from north, east, south, and west, giving the people of Ethiopia today a physical appearance distinct from that of any other people on earth.

Part of the reason for the rich ethnic and cultural heritage of today's Ethiopia is that its boundaries have been in flux for

*A church sexton opens an ancient Coptic bible which grew out of Ethiopia's own distinct forms of Christianity and Judaism.*

*Famine refugees at a camp in Korem in 1984.*

much of the region's history. Ethiopia's boundaries grew and shrank under varying dynasties and individual rulers, as well as through incursions by other neighboring groups into its claimed territory. Its boundaries continue to be disputed even today. Thus, throughout the centuries, different ethnic groups and regions found themselves sometimes part of Ethiopia and sometimes not. Some, such as the Oromo and Tigray, became fully integrated into today's Ethiopia by moving into the heart of its territory, a region known as the western plateau. Over time these groups became politically powerful. Others, such as the Somali and Afar remained rather reluctant Ethiopians and continue to feel alienated even today.

In fact, one of the most hotly debated topics among politically involved Ethiopians today is whether the country was formed by forcing the identity of the historically most powerful group, the Amhara, onto all other groups, or whether the country became over the centuries a true blending of many equal but different cultures. Proponents of the first view believe it is reasonable for groups such as the Tigray and Oromo to press for greater autonomy or even separation from Ethiopia (as Eritrea successfully did in the 1990s). They argue that they were forced to become "Ethiopian" in the first place and that their real identity is important to reclaim. Those who argue the second position see Ethiopians as having a common national identity at this point in their history, and they believe that the country validly exists only as one nation. This conflict in point of view is at the core of much of the political turmoil in Ethiopia today.

## PUZZLES AND PARADOXES

Ethiopia is truly one of the most complex and puzzling places on earth. Its citizens are justifiably proud of the fact that their country is one of only two African nations (Liberia is the other) to have remained independent in the twentieth century while the rest of Africa was colonized by European powers. Though Ethiopians celebrate their past ability to fight off foreign threats, the nation has not as yet sufficiently mobilized to defeat its own internal enemies—underdevelopment of land and industry, and governments that apparently put politics ahead of people. Ethiopia has had many extraordinary leaders, from the legendary Queen of Sheba to Haile Selassie, but the leader of true visionary greatness so desperately needed today has not yet emerged.

Ethiopia is divided between people who wish only to live as they have for centuries, rejecting modernization or outside influences, and those who would like to see the country develop a strong industrial and more stable agricultural base even if it means fundamental changes in society. Without modernization, Ethiopia will continue to lack the ability to live independently of foreign aid and use profits from exports to fund schools, roads, and other projects. Traditionalists are not sure schools or roads are a good idea because both bring about disruption of familiar ways. Neither group seems clear about how to achieve some middle ground—to preserve what is good about the past but still be able to count on a future free of starvation and debilitating poverty.

The eyes of the world will continue to be on Ethiopia, hoping that the tragic images of starving children and helpless adults will give way to a more positive reality. The challenge facing Ethiopia in the twenty-first century will be to rebuild a country with a glorious, fabled past into a powerful and productive modern nation—a nation that nevertheless, because of its unique heritage, will remain unlike any other on earth.

# 1

# LIVING ON THE ROOF OF AFRICA

Ethiopia is often called "the roof of Africa," although a map of the continent demonstrates that this is not really accurate. Ethiopia does not sit atop Africa but rather is approximately a third of the way down the eastern side of the continent. It is, in fact, far closer to the equator, which runs just south of Ethiopia through Kenya, than to the waters of the Mediterranean, which lap the shores of Morocco, Algeria, and Tunisia. It is these three countries that form the actual northern most part of Africa.

However, there is still good reason to speak metaphorically about Ethiopia being Africa's roof because of its relatively high elevation. Most of northern Africa is made up of low-lying regions, the most notable of which is the vast Sahara Desert. Ethiopia, though it too has some areas of low elevation, is primarily comprised of several plateaus and mountain ranges. Thus, though it is nearly surrounded by desert, Ethiopia is startlingly different than neighboring countries. This difference in physical appearance is symbolic of the uniqueness of Ethiopia. It developed over centuries largely as a land apart, cultivating a separate culture even to the extent of having its own alphabet. A visitor looking around nearly any Ethiopian landscape or wandering through any Ethiopian village would not mistake Ethiopia for some other place.

## LOCATION AND BOUNDARIES

Another term used for the part of the continent in which Ethiopia is located is the "Horn of Africa." Northeastern Africa is separated from the Arabian Peninsula by the Red Sea, which at its southern end turns eastward into another

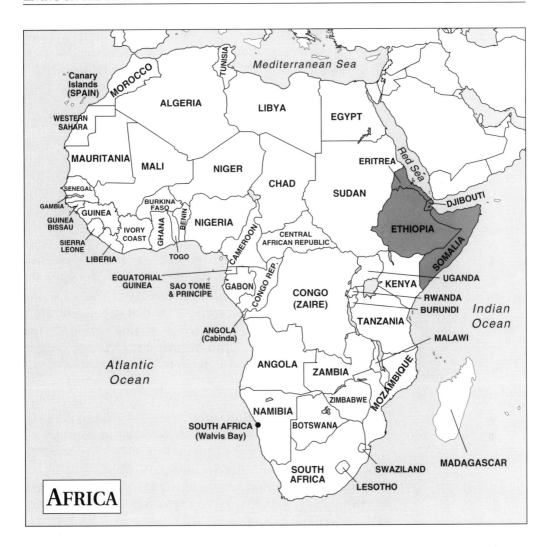

AFRICA

body of water called the Gulf of Aden. On a map the evidence is clear that eons ago the Arabian Peninsula and Africa formed one land mass. The waters of the Gulf of Aden and the Red Sea have now filled in the gap formed when the two continents separated. This separation caused the character-istic "horn" that juts out of the east African coast. Somalia, Djibouti, and Eritrea are the other countries of the horn.

Ethiopia does not occupy any of the region's coastline. In the southern part of the horn, Somalia hugs the entire coast, ex-tending down the eastern shores of Africa to the Kenyan bor-der. The coast along the Red Sea portion of the Horn of Africa belongs to Eritrea, which recently won its independence from

Ethiopia. Between Eritrea and Somalia, the tiny country of Djibouti blocks Ethiopia's access to the remaining small stretch of shoreline. Lack of coastal access has hindered Ethiopia's economic development because it has no ports of its own.

To the west and north of Ethiopia lies the Sudan, which is almost entirely desert. Ethiopia's southern boundary is its border with Kenya. Many of these borders do not have a particularly long history, having been established by European powers early in the twentieth century when they colonized Africa. Some of the borders in the Horn of Africa were actually drawn by a ruler without any apparent concern for the settlement patterns or historical rivalries of those who lived in the region. One example of this is the perfectly straight borderline of one stretch of Ethiopia's boundary with Somalia. Though it might have seemed at the time to be a simple matter of drawing a line across a sparsely inhabited semidesert, such arbitrary borders have created ongoing tension and bloodshed in the Horn of Africa because ethnic groups were either split between two countries or forced to coexist where they had once lived separately.

## THE GREAT RIFT VALLEY

According to the authors of *Ethiopia: A Country Study*, Ethiopia is composed of a "massive highland complex of mountains and dissected plateaus divided by the Great Rift Valley . . . and surrounded by lowlands, steppes, or semidesert."[1] The Great Rift Valley actually extends from the Red Sea through eastern Africa down to Mozambique, but some of its most unusual and scenic stretches are in Ethiopia. The Great Rift Valley serves as a good point of orientation for the various regions of Ethiopia. For example, the western and eastern plateaus are so named because they fall, respectively, to the west and east of the Great Rift Valley. The valley also illustrates a general truth about terrain and climate in regions on or near the equator. In equatorial zones, climate is affected by altitude more than by any other single factor. Because the valley has been carved deeply over the ages by rivers, the elevation is so much lower in the valley that the climate is more like the semideserts of eastern Ethiopia than it is like the regions lying at higher altitude on either side of the valley. Thus, the districts that straddle the valley, notably Tigray and Shewa, have a greater diversity not only of terrain but also of lifestyles and cultures as a result of the widely varying conditions under which people live.

On or near the Great Rift Valley are many of the most memorable sights in Ethiopia, including the Danakil Depression, which at 381 feet below sea level is the lowest point on the earth's land surface. The Rift Valley produces strings of lakes all along its course, and Ethiopia is no exception. Beautiful Lake Abaya and Lake Chamo glitter in the bright sunlight and attract migrating birds and hundreds of other species to their waters and banks. On the border between Ethiopia and Kenya, Lake Turkana glimmers an eerie blue in the midst of the desert.

## THE WESTERN PLATEAU

Though the Great Rift Valley may be one of nature's wonders, it is actually not Ethiopia's most prominent region economically, historically, or culturally. That designation, most would agree, belongs to the western (or Amhara) plateau.

# THE ETHNIC GROUPS OF ETHIOPIA

The Ethiopian people are made up of dozens of ethnic groups speaking many different languages. Of these groups, the Oromo is by far the largest, comprising about half the population. Their original homeland was in the plateaus of south and central Ethiopia, but they have now spread across most of Ethiopia. The Amhara are the second largest group, at approximately 30 percent of the population. They played the lead role in Ethiopian politics for centuries and gave their name, Amharic, to the major language of the country. The Amhara are centered in the western plateau.

The third largest group, the Tigray, are centered in the region of the same name. They speak, Tigrinya, a language related to Amharic. They have risen in political prominence in recent years as a result of their leadership in the effort to get rid of the dictator Mengistu Haile Mariam. The fourth largest group is the Somali, who are concentrated in the Ogaden region of southern Ethiopia. They are the largest Muslim group in Ethiopia.

Other notable groups include the agriculturalist group from the southwestern region, the Sidamo; the Gurage of central Ethiopia near the capital city of Addis Ababa; and the Afar, a nomadic people in the arid northeast, known until recently to greet intruders by cutting off their testicles.

One last group, the Falasha are dwindling in numbers. Called the Beta Israel people, they are the remnants of Ethiopia's long-standing Jewish history and tradition. They are thought to have been in Ethiopia long before the spread of Christianity. In fact, their practices include nothing dating from the period of the Talmud, a sacred Jewish text, indicating that they had split from the mainstream Jewish faith be-

fore the Talmud was written. Many immigrated to Israel in the 1980s and 1990s, some in an airlift in 1991, undertaken by the Jews of Israel to rescue the Falasha from the famine raging in Ethiopia. Fewer than two thousand Falasha remain in Ethiopia today.

*Members of the Falasha display their unique black pottery for sale.*

This is the larger of the two plateau regions and includes the capital, Addis Ababa, most of Ethiopia's major historic sites, and almost all of the best agricultural land.

Of the thirteen administrative divisions that make up Ethiopia today, the regions of Gonder, Gojam, Welega, Iluba-bor, Kefa, and Gema Gema are entirely on the western plateau. Parts of Tigray, Welo, and Shewa are also on the plateau, but these districts straddle the Great Rift Valley to the east and continue into other geographic areas. Though much of Ethiopia is sparsely populated, most Ethiopians live some-where in the western plateau, including the 1.5 million resi-dents of Addis Ababa, in the Shewa district. Two of the four smaller cities in Ethiopia, Gonder and Dese, with populations of around 70,000 each, also are on the western plateau.

The region is characterized by rugged terrain. Mountain ranges such as the Choke and Simyen Mountains have peaks as high as fifteen thousand feet. Between mountain peaks lie flatter lands, which are at an elevation of eight thousand feet or more and are where the most fertile land in Ethiopia lies. These mountain valleys receive enough rain during the year to avoid the need for irrigation and thus are the easiest lands to farm. They are also the most pleasant regions to inhabit be-cause of the mild climate typical of higher elevations near the equator.

## GONDER

Gonder, sometimes spelled *Gondar,* is the northernmost re-gion of Ethiopia entirely on the western plateau. It is one of the most historically significant and geographically magnif-icent regions of the country. It is home to the Simyen Moun-tains, capped by Ras Dashen, which at 15,158 feet, is the highest elevation in the country and the fourth-highest peak in Africa. The Simyen Mountains are home to much unique wildlife, including the Simyen wolf, the rarest canine species in the world.

Ethiopians call the mountain regions *dega,* to distinguish them from the lower elevations of this region, which are called *wayna dega.* In the regions known as *dega,* snow is common, and frost can occur most of the year. The land is too high to be suitable for cultivation, and thus the *dega* is very sparsely populated. In the *wayna dega,* temperatures are comfortable year round, typically hovering around seventy degrees Fahrenheit, with seasons demarcated more by patterns of rainfall than by temperature. The rainy season gets off to a start with a period of short rains, called *belg*, from March through May. Then the rains begin in earnest in the middle of June, with the season known as *keremt*, which generally lasts until September. The rest of the year is dry. In most years the plateaus will receive about forty inches of rain; however, many seasons of drought in a row are common, bringing on the famines that are now one of the facts of life in Ethiopia.

The city of Gonder has given its name to the entire region. Gonder was founded in 1635 by Emperor Fasil (sometimes called Fasiladas), who thought that a permanent capital city might bring stability to a country wracked by religious conflicts and regional quarrels. It remained the capital for 250 years. According to travel writer Philip Briggs, "Gonder today is one of Ethiopia's largest and most impressive cities."[2] Two of the most important sights in Gonder are the Royal Enclosure and King Fasil's Pool, both built during the time of Fasil. The Royal Enclosure has five castles connected by tunnels and raised walkways, all enclosed by a high stone wall. King Fasil's Pool is about a mile out of town. It is a large sunken bathing pool overlooked by a two-story building thought to have been one of Fasil's homes. Another famous sight in Gonder is the beautiful church of Debre Birhan Selassie, said to contain one of the most beautiful examples of Ethiopian art: a painted ceiling of angel faces that stare down at visitors.

## LAKE TANA

Located partly in Gonder, along its border with Gojam, is Lake Tana, the source of a portion of the Nile River known as the Blue Nile. Lake Tana covers approximately fourteen hundred square miles and is by far the largest lake in Ethiopia. Lake Tana is famous for several sights that can be seen from its banks. The first is the large number of papyrus fishing boats, called *tankwa*, still made in a style similar to that of ancient Egypt. Papyrus is the material from which paper was originally made (and from which it got its name). Because it becomes waterlogged fairly quickly, these boats are only temporary.

The second interesting thing about Lake Tana is the number of monasteries on its islands. One of these, Dago Istafanos,

## DEBRE BIRHAN SELASSIE

Although there are more than forty churches in Gonder, only seven date from the time of Fasil, founder of the capital there, and six of these were severely damaged when Gonder was attacked by the army of the dervish of Sudan during Ethiopia's nineteenth-century war with that country. Debre Birhan Selassie is the only church to have survived this war intact. Ethiopian tradition says that the church's salvation came about through the miraculous intervention of a swarm of bees.

Debre Birhan Selassie, which means "the Trinity" in Amharic, is best known for its roof, from which eighty painted faces look down on worshipers. Its walls are also painted with portraits of saints and other religious events. The outside of the church has twelve towers, representing the twelve apostles. The gateway looks like a lion resting on its belly, with a tail that curves up and becomes part of the carvings on the front of the building itself. The lion is meant to represent Christ, and throughout the church complex other similarly symbolic references abound.

Historians believe that Fasil's successor, Yohannes I, planned to bring the Ark of the Covenant to Gonder and house it in this church. Although other churches in the Gonder area are round, Debre Birhan Selassie is rectangular, designed to the same specifications as Solomon's Temple in Jerusalem, the original repository of the alleged ark. The original foundation, however, is round, indicating that Yohannes deliberately ordered changes to make the church unique when he got the idea to house the ark there.

has a mausoleum in which the mummified remains of five Ethiopian kings are displayed in glass coffins. Another is Tana Kirkos. There, according to tradition, the legendary Ark of the Covenant (allegedly containing the original stone tablets of the Ten Commandments) was kept for eight hundred years before its removal to Aksum (known today as Axum) in northeastern Ethiopia in the fourth century A.D.

### GOJAM AND THE BLUE NILE

The Blue Nile emerges from the southern end of Lake Tana, in the administrative district called Gojam. The river is an ideal habitat for the hippopotamuses and crocodiles that can

*Also called "Smoke of the Nile," the Blue Nile Falls is one of the most spectacular waterfalls in the world.*

be seen lounging on its banks. It is also the site, about twenty miles downstream, of the spectacular Blue Nile Falls, called Tis Abay, or "Smoke of the Nile," by Ethiopians. Reputed to be one of the most spectacular waterfalls in the world, Tis Abay is formed from a number of streams that are channeled into a narrow, deep gorge below the falls. According to Philip Briggs, "This truly magnificent gorge is . . . comparable in scale to America's Grand Canyon."[3] The Blue Nile meanders in a long curve through the region, forming the boundary between Gojam and the administrative district of Welega, before it leaves Ethiopia to continue its journey across the Sudan. There it joins the Nile River, known in this region as the White Nile.

## WESTERN AND SOUTHWESTERN ETHIOPIA

The four administrative districts of Welega, Ilubabor, Kefa, and Gema Gema compose the west and southwest corner of Ethiopia. This area is characterized by rolling hills and nearly impenetrable forests. Large tracts of land are cultivated, however, with coffee being a major regional crop. Some linguists claim that the word for coffee is derived from the word *Kefa*, and experts generally agree that Ethiopia is the original source of the coffee bean.

One of the most interesting parts of this remote region of Ethiopia is a town and national park both named Gambella. The park is a swampy region, full of exotic birds, crocodiles, hippos, and monkeys. Both park and town are located along the Baro River, a tributary of the Nile that defines the border between the Welega and Ilubabor districts. According to Philip Briggs, the town of Gambella "exudes an atmosphere of tropical languor, dictated as much by its lush vegetation and almost unbearable humidity as by its remoteness from just about everywhere. This powerful sense of place is underscored by the brown waters of the wide Baro River . . . which rolls lazily past the town."[4]

Because the Baro River is navigable as far as the city of Khartoum in the Sudan, the tiny port town of Gambella, which might otherwise have remained in what Briggs calls its "tropical languor," has had a remarkably turbulent history. Founded in 1907 and passed between Britain, Italy, and the Sudan throughout the first half of the twentieth century, Gambella became part of Ethiopia in 1957. Turbulence continues today because of tensions between two local ethnic groups. One of these is the numerically larger pastoralist (or herding) group, the Nuer, who are fairly new arrivals to the region. The other is the Anuwak, who are the long-standing inhabitants of the region and make their living primarily by fishing. Sudanese who feel the region belongs in the Sudan also contribute to the tension by their armed incursions into the region.

## ARUSI, BALE, AND SIDAMO

The districts of Arusi, Bale, and Sidamo lie in southern Ethiopia on the eastern side of the Rift Valley and together make up what is known as the eastern (or Somali) plateau. In most respects, the eastern plateau is very much like the western plateau. High mountains abound in the two ranges known as Mendebo and Ahmar, and fertile valleys suitable for agriculture attract permanent settlements.

However, only Arusi is completely on the plateau. What characterizes this southern region of Ethiopia in Bale and

Sidamo is a gradual downward slope from the plateau into semidesert. Here the population is smaller because the land is difficult to cultivate, and as one approaches the border with Kenya the environment is increasingly hotter and more forbidding to all but the pastoralist groups who tend their herds in the area.

## HARER

The southeastern region of Ethiopia is known as Harer. The southern part of this district juts eastward into a point, following roughly the shape of the Horn of Africa. This region, called the Ogaden, is the home of many Somali nomads. Largely arid, it has few natural resources, is too dry to be widely cultivated, and contains few permanent communities. Still, the Ogaden is the source of great controversy and tension between Somalia and Ethiopia. Many Somali are committed to the idea of a Greater Somalia, which would comprise all areas where ethnic Somali live in large

*An open-air market is held near a mosque in Harer in southeastern Ethiopia.*

## "RAMBO'S HOUSE"

According to travel writer Philip Briggs, in *Guide to Ethiopia,*

> Harer was an important centre of Muslim trade and learning throughout the 17th and 18th centuries. Only Muslims were allowed to enter its walls, and as a result its location was the source of more rumour than substance in the Christian world. The first European to visit the city was the British explorer Richard Burton who, in 1854, spent ten anxious days there, unsure whether he was a guest or prisoner of the Emir.

The exotic reputation of this remote, fabled city attracted another famous nineteenth-century visitor, the French poet Arthur Rimbaud. Rimbaud, who abandoned writing poetry at the age of 19, moved to Harer in 1880, and was a trader in the region until he died in 1891.

Visitors to Harer looking for the link to Rimbaud will be directed to "Rambo's House," the spelling that most closely approximates the way locals say the poet's name. The house is interesting particularly for its frescoes, which locals say Rimbaud himself painted. However, according to Briggs, the house is probably not authentically linked to the poet but simply "the house that was used to film a movie about Rimbaud—and no, Sylvester Stallone didn't play the lead."

numbers. Somalia would like its country's border to go roughly straight across Harer, thus subsuming the pointed portion of Ethiopia altogether. Until recently, when Eritrean troops crossed the Ethiopian border, setting off a threat of war, no border in the Horn of Africa has been more hotly contested than this one.

Nearly bisecting Harer is the Ahmar Mountain range, also called the Arba Gugu Mountains. High in these mountains is the historic city of Harer, after which the district is named. According to writer Philip Briggs, "The walled city of Harer, the spiritual heart of Ethiopia's large Muslim community, is considered by Muslims to be the fourth holiest city in the world."[5] Founded in the twelfth century, it became a significant force in Ethiopia in the sixteenth century, when it was used as the base from which Muslims launched their attacks on Ethiopia's Christian empire. The walls were built during the mid–sixteenth century not to keep out Christians, but to defend against the Oromo of southern Ethiopia, who were using the distraction of the Muslim-Christian hostilities as an opportunity to expand their own territory.

Near Harer, on the northern slope of the Ahmar Mountains is the town of Dire Dawa, the second most populous city in Ethiopia. It was founded in 1902 when a railway—today still Ethiopia's only rail service—was built to link Addis Ababa with the port of Djibouti. From Dire Dawa, the Ahmar Mountains drop steeply into the Rift Valley, which in this area is very hot and arid. Some relief from the heat can be found along the banks of the Awash River, which flows through this part of the valley. In recent years dams have been built on the Awash to create new sources of hydroelectric power and to provide means for irrigating local farms. Being able to increase arable farmland is an important part of creating larger and more reliable zones of agriculture to feed Ethiopia's people.

## WELO AND TIGRAY

The two districts of Welo (or Wolo) and Tigray (or Tigre) make up the northeastern corner of Ethiopia. These two regions are home to some of the most important cultural and historic sites in Ethiopia, and Tigray is the site of one of its most remarkable geographic wonders, the Danakil Depression. This below-sea-level region is one of the most challenging places on earth to live, but it has been home for centuries to the Afar, a nomadic group that makes a living cutting salt blocks and carrying them to distant markets.

The ancient capital of Aksum, which predates the birth of Christ by several centuries, is in Tigray. Today the city of Axum (its modern name) is most noted for a unique field of stelae, or stone monoliths. These were erected by ancient kings as a means of showing their might. The largest standing stela (the singular form of stelae) is attributed to King Ezanas. It is over seventy feet high and was carved from a solid block of granite that was quarried approximately three miles away and probably brought by elephants to Aksum. An even larger stela weighing five hundred tons lies broken on the ground. If erect, it would be approximately

## THE DANAKIL DEPRESSION

"The hell-hole of creation" is the way one early European explorer described the Danakil Depression, according to Curt Stager's *National Geographic* article, "Africa's Great Rift." Partly in Ethiopia and partly in neighboring Djibouti, the Danakil Depression is an area along the Great Rift where the earth's crust has stretched and thinned and the land has sunk over time to 371 feet below sea level, the lowest point on earth's land surface. Here the earth's crust is thin enough that new land surface is constantly being created by new lava that oozes upward. Water also seeps down, to be ejected again as steam. Volcanic cones are common sights, as are deep cracks in the earth. Hundreds of small earthquakes convulse the area every year. The temperature is so hot that ordinary thermometers cannot register the upper limit, which can exceed 120 degrees Fahrenheit.

The landscape is garishly colored with bright oranges, greens, yellows, and blues from the various mineral deposits left behind by evaporating water. Salt crystallizes into perfect cubes that collect in eerie geometric shapes around small vent holes in the earth. Astonishingly, the nomadic Afar people actually find a home here, collecting and selling the evaporated salt that forms on the surface. The region where the Danakil Depression is located is called the Afar Triangle after these hardy people.

one hundred feet high. It is credited with being, in the words of historian B. R. Buxton in *The Abyssinians,* "probably the largest single block of stone ever quarried, carved, and set up in the ancient world."[6]

Also in Axum is the church of St. Mary of Zion, where the supposed Ark of the Covenant is held under heavy protection. In another part of Tigray is the Debre Damo monastery, a sixth-century stone church built, without the benefit of modern technology, on top of a cliff from stones quarried elsewhere. Access can be gained only by what author and photographer Kazuyoshi Nomachi calls a "hair raising 49-foot perpendicular climb . . . assisted by a rope pulled from the summit by friendly monks."[7] Eastern Tigray has well over one hundred rock churches, mostly carved into cliff faces, probably dating from the sixth to tenth centuries. According to Philip Briggs, "The mountainous sandstone rockscapes of

Tigre have an angular, wild quality quite distinct from the more curvaceous green hills seen elsewhere in the Ethiopian highlands."[8] Stone terraces built for irrigation, and orderly stone villages contribute to the distinctive look of the region. Welo has a similar appearance to Tigray and contains a number of sites of equal historic importance, including the ancient center of Lalibela. Lalibela, an isolated mountain town famous for its rock-hewn churches, was originally called Roha but was renamed in honor of King Lalibela, who was responsible for initiating the carving of the churches. According to legend, a very young Lalibela was covered by a swarm of bees, which was taken as an omen that he would one day rule the region. The word *Lalibela* means "the bees recognize his sovereignty."

Once he was crowned he began building churches in an unusual style. Rather than building up from the ground, rock was

*Axum's stone monoliths called stelae were erected by ancient kings to symbolize their might.*

carved down so that the churches actually are below ground level in stone pits. Some of the churches are more than thirty feet high and are reached by tunnels. According to Briggs,

*This rock-hewn church in Lalibela is carved below ground level.*

> If you wander between the churches in the thin light of morning, when white-robed hermits emerge bible-in-hand from their cells to bask on the rocks, and the chill highland air is warmed by . . . drumbeats and gentle swaying chants, you can't help but feel that you are witnessing a scene that is fundamentally little different to the one that has been enacted here every morning for century upon century.[9]

## SHEWA AND ADDIS ABABA

Worlds apart from the calm of Lalibela is the capital city of Addis Ababa in the province of Shewa (or Shoa). Situated approximately seven thousand feet above sea level, it is the third highest capital city in the world and enjoys a mild climate year round. Addis Ababa is typical of many third-world cities in that it is a rather overwhelming blend of noise, chaotic construction, unregulated traffic, and what seems to be relentless human misery. Still, for its residents, Addis Ababa presents opportunities to make a living and enjoy—or at least dream about enjoying—a higher standard of living than is possible in the remote villages and small towns of rural Ethiopia.

The city was founded in 1887 by Emperor Menelik II, who gave it the name "New Flower," or Addis Ababa. Its commercial center is the Mercato, a marketplace reputedly the largest on the continent. Stretching for many square blocks, it is comprised of stalls and small shops selling a little bit of everything—spices, souvenirs, vegetables, jewelry, and bootleg compact discs. The city is also famous for its National Museum, one of the best in Africa, which displays priceless artifacts from all eras of Ethiopian history. Its greatest claim to fame is the skull of "Lucy," whose discovery in 1974 revealed that the ancestors of human beings inhabited Africa at least 3.5 million years ago—at least 2.5 million years earlier than had been previously thought.

Ethiopia is a land of majestic scenery and awe-inspiring ancient monuments. It is home also to many fiercely independent and distinct ethnic groups. It is a land of mystery, full of history largely unknown in the west—a country that will not quickly reveal its secrets and that only recently has encouraged outsiders to visit. Still, those who wish to learn about this complex land will be rewarded, for it is truly one of the most unusual places on earth.

# From Lucy to the Twentieth Century

Four million years ago the Afar region was a lake surrounded by green valleys. As the waters retreated, the hot and forbidding environment of today's Danakil Depression emerged. Emerging along with it were fossil beds from the marshes surrounding the lake, where in 1974, a team of Ethiopian, European, and American anthropologists made a discovery that changed forever our understanding of the origins of humanity. There in the desert were the bones of a three-foot-high, approximately sixty-pound female figure who had lived 3.4 million years ago. It was clearly a human ancestor; it walked upright, and though its arms were longer, suited for climbing in trees, it had a distinctly human appearance. They gave the nearly intact skeleton several names. *Australopithecus afarensis* is its species name, named after the region of Afar, but it is better known to Ethiopians as Dinquinesh, or "thou art wonderful." The rest of the world knows the skeleton as Lucy, after the Beatles' song "Lucy in the Sky with Diamonds," which was popular among the team camped at the site.

The almost incomprehensible age of Lucy gives a new twist to the words "ancient" and "modern." Usually people describe any period before the beginning of the Christian era as ancient history, but even the earliest recorded history is only a few thousand years old, truly only a blink of an eye. However, millions of years after Lucy, it is clear that East Africa has remained in the forefront of human history, for it is here that some of the great civilizations of the past also rose and fell.

## AKSUM

By the eighth millennium B.C., the human ancestors of today's Ethiopians were domesticating and herding cattle, goats, and sheep. By the third millennium B.C., they were cultivating thirty-six crops, including teff, a small grain, and *ensete*, a plant called "false banana," whose pulp is mashed for bread or porridge. Both of these crops are still staples of the Ethiopian diet today. By the second millennium B.C., they were using plows to clear land and engaging in trade with other regions, particularly the Sudan and the Arabian Peninsula. From this era can be traced the beginnings of a distinctly Ethiopian culture, influenced

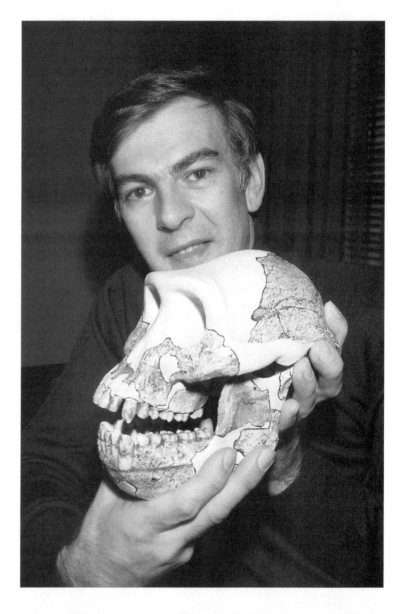

*An anthropologist holds the skull of Lucy, a three-foot-high human ancestor discovered in 1974 in the Afar region of Ethiopia.*

## GE'EZ

The Aksumite empire created the only indigenous African alphabet and form of script, used to write the language known as Ge'ez. Today, Amharic and the other languages of Ethiopia still use a unique alphabet derived from Ge'ez. As a written language, Ge'ez evolved in a curious manner, being first written in what is called a boustrophedon style. This literally means "as the ox turns in plowing," and refers to script that is not written left to right, or right to left, but in alternating directions from line to line, similar to the way a field is plowed. This system was eventually abandoned in favor of writing left to right, as in English. Known as the Latin of Africa, Ge'ez today exists only in holy texts read by monks.

greatly by exposure to traditions and practices of south Arabia, particularly the area known as Saba, or Sheba.

By 500 B.C., well organized societies and small kingdoms were competing for power, land, and wealth in the Horn of Africa. The most successful of these competing groups was the one centered around Aksum, a five- to eight-day caravan trip inland from the major port at Adulis. Numerous references in books written at the time and the existence of minted coins from the Aksumite kingdom support the claim that Ethiopia was at this point one of the world's most advanced cultures. On a par with Egypt, Persia, and Rome as a trading power, Aksum controlled trade into the Sudan and thus was the link to all of inland northeast Africa.

### CHRISTIANS, JEWS AND MUSLIMS

Ethiopia began its long and unique Christian history in the fourth century A.D., when, according to tradition, two shipwrecked young Syrians, Frumentius and Aedisius, were brought to Aksum as slaves of the king, Ella Amida. Over the years the two young men impressed the king and his court with their wisdom and character. Eventually freed upon the death of Ella Amida, they were asked to stay because the monarch had a young son, Ezanas, whom his widow wished to have educated as a Christian. Ezanas became an important ruler himself, pushing the boundaries of the Aksumite empire westward and southward into today's Sudan and establishing Aksum as the unquestioned

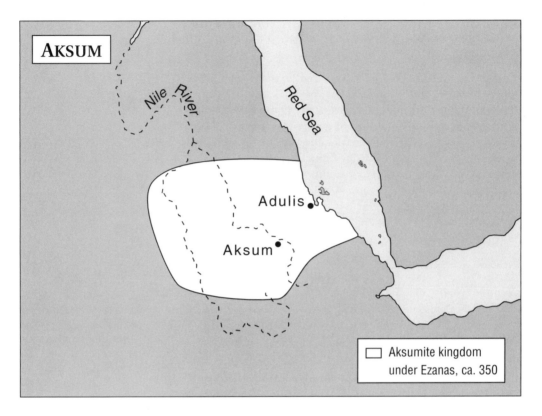

power in the Horn of Africa, the only Christian kingdom outside Europe.

Judaism, despite being a far older religion, actually came to Ethiopia later than Christianity did. Since about the sixth century, groups of Falasha, or "black Jews," have lived in isolated communities in the area around Gonder. A few centuries later, a third and far more significant religious force, Islam, first came to Aksum. Early Muslims quickly established themselves as the great sea power of the eastern Mediterranean and Red Sea. Aksum remained Christian when most of the neighboring countries were converting to Islam, and thus it found itself isolated and unable to sustain its trade routes through its ports because of hostile Islamic patrols on the Red Sea.

To prevent a loss of power in light of new Muslim dominance, Aksum turned inland, expanding its base deeper south into what is now southern Ethiopia. Drained by constant battle with local ethnic groups who resisted incorporation into Aksum, the mighty empire soon found itself in deep trouble with another enemy as well—drought. According to historian John Reader, "Beginning around A.D. 750, the region's difficulties were exacerbated by a decline in annual rainfall," soon reducing agriculture to "the single season which had prevailed before Aksum rose to wealth and power."[10] Aksum was unable to feed its population, which gradually drifted southward into central Ethiopia to farm in areas that had not been depleted by overplanting and grazing. The fall of the Aksumite empire came when the Jewish warrior queen Judith (or Yodit) with her army of Falasha, sacked the city of Aksum in the ninth century, toppling the tall monuments characteristic of the kingdom. Although the exact dates are not known, she reigned for approximately the next forty years.

## THE ZAGWE DYNASTY

Aksumite attempts to maintain power through expansion inland had already laid groundwork for a new dynasty even before Yodit came to power. As the Aksumite empire pushed outward, it came into contact with the Agew, another Christian group, who were enlisted by the Aksumites into their army and brought into the life of the court. Little by little the cultures intermingled and the Agew became accustomed to their new prestige. Eventually, after a period of several generations following Yodit's death, when the region had no central authority, the Agew were able to establish themselves as the emperors of a dynasty that called itself the Zagwe.

Information about the Zagwe dynasty, which lasted about 150 years beginning in the middle of the twelfth century, is sketchy and conflicting. After the fall of the Zagwe in 1270, Yekuno Amlak, another ruler claiming descent from Solomon, took the throne, and a systematic attempt to downplay the Zagwe period was undertaken. As historian

*A depiction of the Jewish warrior queen, Judith, who is believed to have sacked the city of Aksum in the ninth century.*

# THE DESCENDANTS OF KING SOLOMON

According to legend, the Queen of Sheba (so named because of her origins in southern Arabia, but actually a resident of the Aksumite empire) traveled to Jerusalem in the tenth century to meet King Solomon, learn about Jewish culture, and improve relationships between the two powers. When she was about to leave, she made a wager with Solomon that if she could not spend her last night there without taking anything that was his, she would sleep with him. In the middle of the night she woke with a raging thirst and took a drink of water. Solomon claimed that the water was his and thus demanded that she keep her end of the bargain. She did, and returned to Aksum pregnant with his child, who eventually became Emperor Menelik I. It was as a result of this liaison that the supposed Ark of the Covenant was allegedly brought to Ethiopia soon after.

It was also as a result of the birth of Menelik that the rulers of Ethiopia through most of its subsequent history, down to its last emperor Haile Selassie, have claimed lineage back to the fabled King Solomon. Skeptics point to the fact that the story of Solomon and Sheba was not actually written down until the fourteenth century, at the time when the descendants of Menelik had regained the throne after the Zagwe dynasty. The story is told in an important historic text called the *Kebre Negast*. This lends support to the view that the stories are at least in part a fabrication designed to give the monarchy a dazzling, historic past, with famous lineage dating from the liaison between Solomon and the Queen of Sheba. However, although details may be greatly embellished, it is historical fact that communication between Jerusalem and Aksum was established and remained strong during this era.

*Solomon meets the Queen of Sheba. Legend holds that a liaison between them produced the emperor Menelik I.*

Harold G. Marcus observes, "The Zagwes have been derided in Solomonic chronicles and their achievements obscured. Even at the height of their rule, churchmen considered them usurpers."[11] Biased, fabricated, and distorted versions of this part of Ethiopian history have come down through the centuries and have made an accurate history of this era difficult to write.

However, one great legacy of the Zagwe dynasty remains: the churches of Lalibela. According to Marcus, "In order physically to demonstrate the primacy of the new order over the Axumite line, Emperor Lalibela (1185–1225) directed the building of eleven rock-hewn churches at his capital at Roha (now Lalibela)."[12] Ironically, it was not until the last few decades that the number, scale, and size of the rock churches of the Zagwe era have been unearthed and the accomplishment appreciated by Ethiopians and the world.

## THE RETURN OF THE SOLOMONIC LINE

In 1270 Yekuno Amlak, a descendant of the original rulers claiming kinship to Solomon, reclaimed the throne for his family. For the first few generations, the ruling family was intent upon building its own royal stature. Monarchs adopted the title of *negusa nagast* (king of kings), ruling over regional kings, each of whom was known as a *ras*. Farmers and other citizens were required to pay taxes and to show deference to the monarch by not looking at him when he passed and by kissing the ground when he spoke. Monarchs traveled with large numbers of servants, sometimes accompanied by chained lions to show their power. There was no capital city; rather, the capital was considered to be wherever the monarch was. Like contemporaries in European

*The church of St. Abba Libanos in Lalibela is a legacy of the Zagwe dynasty.*

countries, the monarchy thrived on exploiting a sense of mystery about its comings and goings, showed its great wealth by elaborate ceremonies and parades, and demonstrated the extent of its riches by throwing gold, food, and other valuable commodities to passersby.

Such efforts were not entirely selfish. A strong monarch was an important part of building confidence in a nation. However, the Solomonic rulers' goal was not so much to become a world power as simply to ensure that Ethiopia was not overrun by outsiders. Ethiopia's ruling class was deeply committed to Christianity, and the country valued its unique cultural institutions. Thus, Ethiopian rulers did not focus so much on conquering vast new territories but rather turned inward, concentrating on developing a cohesive and united country.

## AMDA SIYON

Intent on regaining what had previously been part of, or at least under the influence of the first Solomonic rulers, the newly restored ruling family moved against rival ethnic groups such as the Tigray on the western plateau, and they stationed army legions in border regions to the south. They also established their language, Amharic, as the one spoken by the elite. Of particular note is the great Emperor Amda Siyon, who ruled from 1314 to 1344. He claimed all land as his own, then essentially leased it back as *gults,* or fiefs, to local nobles and successful generals. Those so favored could maintain their high status in their regions only by declaring loyalty to the emperor; supplying soldiers, crops, and animals on demand; and collecting taxes from farmers. This system was similar to that in place at the same time in western Europe.

Over time, however, a sense of hereditary right grew. Later emperors found they could no longer enforce the idea that they alone had the right to bestow a *gult* because fathers felt that they had the right to pass lands on to their sons. In outlying regions, local rulers became more confident of their own power and more willing to challenge the emperor's authority. This was to play a significant role in later history. At the time, however, Amda Siyon was more concerned about the existence of a strong Muslim presence in what is today eastern Ethiopia. Fearing that a Muslim stronghold would threaten the stability of the entire region, Amda Siyon moved quickly and decisively. In 1316, shortly after taking the throne, the emperor attacked and conquered Yifat, a Muslim community near Shewa, forcing residents to pay taxes in tribute.

Within a few years Muslims struck back, taking advantage of the fact that Amda Siyon was preoccupied with putting down local insurrections in Tigray and elsewhere. In 1332, Sabradin, the ruler of Yifat, declared a holy war against Amda Siyon. Amda Siyon saw that a thorough defeat of Muslim forces would create the overall security in the region he had been hoping for, and he rose to the occasion. According to historian Harold G. Marcus, "He led his forces brilliantly, feinting here, probing there, attacking the weakest units in the Muslim federation, and never permitting his enemy to counter in a mass attack. [This] resourceful man . . . mastered and united an empire around him."[13]

## ZARA YAKOB

The growth in power of the Solomonic rulers from the time of Amda Siyon was tied to their role as defenders of

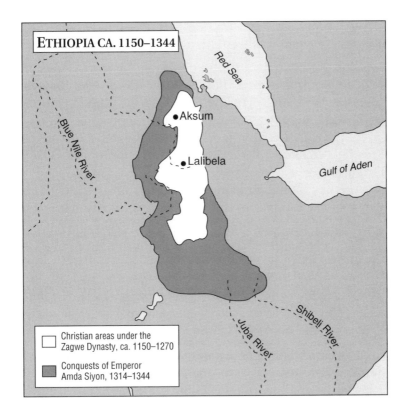

Christianity. In the generations that followed, the church grew in power but split into warring factions. Though disagreement on religious points was theoretically the cause of the divisiveness, the struggle was also over which group would dominate Ethiopian Christianity. In time, Emperor Zara Yakob, who ruled from 1434 to 1468, was able to effect a compromise, and he ensured the cooperation of varying factions by embarking on a huge program of church building and endowments of monasteries.

Zara Yakob was another great Solomonic ruler, who was able through his powers as a statesman to build a stronger nation around two central ideas—Christianity and a political system based on a strong king and loyal subjects. He was also an excellent military leader. Concerned that Muslim forces in the eastern lowlands blocked his kingdom's access to the sea, he moved into what is today Eritrea and established ports along that stretch of the Red Sea. Additionally, he had a view of the world beyond Ethiopia's immediate borders. He established contact with European leaders, inviting them to send emissaries to visit his kingdom.

Many of the rulers of the first two centuries after the reestablishment of the Solomonic line were exceptionally capable. This can be attributed to the Ethiopian system of choosing a monarch. Although there was a royal lineage, there was no tradition of handing down the monarchy from parent to child. It was enough that the monarch be a member of the extended family, so as to continue the Solomonic line. This enabled a committee of church leaders and other ranking citizens to consider many options and choose the person they thought had the best leadership potential. This worked well in terms of choosing the leader, but it created constant intrigue among the extended royal family, all of whom could cherish dreams of becoming emperor or resent the fact that they had not been chosen.

However, the problem with this system was bigger than simply making the committee's choice of monarch stick. The time and infighting involved in choosing a new leader undermined the Ethiopian state. According to Harold G. Marcus,

> Whenever there was a crisis, or, indeed, royal instability, death or succession, the state began to contract. Even in the heartland, political squabbling often

eroded the fragile unities of religion, language, tradition, economics, and mythology. Most of Ethiopia's
peoples continued to think locally, and, for them, the
state was at best a shadowy entity that manifested itself
only in its demand for taxes.[14]

## THE DECLINE OF THE SOLOMONIC EMPIRE

It became apparent, as the quality of leaders diminished after Zara Yakob, that the Solomonic state was becoming
even more shadowy and less of an entity than ever. The op-
posite was happening in the Muslim regions to the east,
where a charismatic Muslim, Ahmad Gran ("the left
handed"), was whipping up sentiments against the Christian kingdom of Ethiopia. He dazzled his audiences with his
rhetoric and soon led an army, the first in the region to
carry firearms, into the Ethiopian highlands. The Christians
were routed in 1528 at the Battle of Shimbra Kure, and from
there Ahmad Gran's army swept through Ethiopia at will,
destroying villages and demolishing churches and other
cultural landmarks.

The conflict was not over, however. Emperor Lebna Dengel went into hiding and from there sent a message to the
Portuguese, asking for assistance in fighting the Muslims and
restoring Christianity to Ethiopia. This call for help unleashed something that resembled a sixteenth-century world
war. It took the Portuguese until 1541 to arrive, and they immediately began training Tigray and other Christians in tech-
niques of European warfare. Ahmad was defeated later in
1541 by a combined and well-armed Portuguese and
Ethiopian army, and he turned for assistance to the sultan of
Turkey, an enemy of Portugal and at the time the most powerful Muslim leader. Turkey provided nine hundred merce-
nary soldiers armed with muskets, and in 1542 this army
slaughtered the Portuguese Christian forces, beheading their
leader Christopher da Gama, son of the famous explorer
Vasco da Gama.

The conflict still was not over. Emperor Galewedos, who
ruled from 1540 to 1559, tried an approach akin to modern
guerrilla warfare. Using a decentralized army divided into
small attack squads, Galewedos struck seemingly at random,
defeating and demoralizing the Muslim army. Finally, the

## THE EUROPEAN CONNECTION

Many people wrongly believe that in past centuries Africa was isolated from the rest of the world and ignorant of Europe's existence. This is not the case. According to eminent historian John Reader, author of a new history of Africa entitled *Africa: A Biography of the Continent,*

> In considering the relationship between Africa and Europe, received wisdom suggests that Africa was a dark and passive continent . . . awaiting the enlightenment that European discovery and exploration ultimately would bring. The truth is otherwise. Far from being passive, Africa responded vigorously to European attempts to establish a presence on the continent; furthermore, Ethiopians were exploring the city streets of Europe long before Europeans visited Ethiopia or any other part of sub-Saharan Africa. The first European to visit Ethiopia was an Italian, Pietro Rombulo, who made the journey in 1407; Ethiopians had visited Italy in 1306—101 years earlier.

> Ample evidence exists that the Italians were not the only Europeans who knew of Ethiopia. In England, Elizabethan literature contains references to Ethiopia, and European paintings of the same period feature some black faces. Interestingly, these references are not tinged with the kind of racism and sense of white superiority that crept into European culture later. In this era, blacks were simply seen as exotic and different. It was only later, with the onset of the Atlantic slave trade, that blacks were portrayed as degenerate or inferior, thus justifying their subjugation by whites.

Muslims withdrew, leaving the highlands once more to the Christians. According to Harold G. Marcus, "The country had lost hundreds of thousands of lives, a measure of confidence in itself and its religion, and much of its capital."[15] Muslims remaining in the empire were bitter, Christians were no longer dazzled by their Solomonic rulers, and other groups were waiting in the wings to seize power.

### THE RISE OF THE OROMO

One of these groups was the Oromo, pastoralists who originally inhabited the lowland regions of southern Ethiopia, but who by the thirteenth century had begun encroaching onto the highland plateaus to find more hospitable grazing land. In the generations that followed, the Oromo took advantage of the Solomonic empire's war-related losses and distractions and gradually became the dominant ethnic group in many parts of Ethiopia. The Oromo were difficult to characterize culturally because they tended to be very adaptable. Traditionally pagan, many converted when they settled in Christian or Muslim areas. Traditionally pastoralists, many became farmers when the opportunity arose. Others kept to the old ways, but little by little, they became an integral part of the social mix wherever they settled. Today the Oromo are the largest and most widespread ethnic group in Ethiopia.

They were indirectly assisted in their rise to prominence by one emperor, Sarsa Dengel, who ruled from 1563 to 1597. To ensure the defense of his empire, Sarsa Dengel decided to reduce its size. He concentrated on developing a well-defended state on the western plateau to the Red Sea, encompassing the regions from today's Shewa northeast through Eritrea. This region became known as Abyssinia. Whereas the term "Ethiopia" had always been somewhat abstract, Abyssinia referred more specifically to the core territory of the Solomonic empire. However, in part because boundaries were so flexible, the terms Abyssinia and Ethiopia were and still are used more or less interchangeably by historians in discussing this period.

Despite the reduced size of Abyssinia, says Harold G. Marcus, "The Christians never forgot that their rulers once held sway over a much larger state."[16] The abstract concept of a Greater Ethiopia remained a powerful source of pride and yearning in Abyssinia, particularly among church leaders. They vehemently opposed what they saw as Sarsa Dengel's abandonment of Christian territory to two infidel groups, the Oromo and the Muslims. Church and state began working at odds, and the ensuing instability would usher in a new period of strife.

## REENTER THE EUROPEANS

The Solomonic emperors had for generations been interested in contact with the west, and by the mid–sixteenth century Portuguese and Spaniards had begun coming to Ethiopia, primarily as missionaries. Though their targets were already Christian, the missionaries hoped to persuade them to abandon Ethiopian Christianity in favor of Roman

Catholicism. It briefly seemed possible when the Emperor Susenyos, who ruled from 1607 to 1632, converted. However, Susenyos then tried to convert the rest of his kingdom forcibly. Resistance, even in the form of group suicides by monks, was massive. Civil war broke out, and when Susenyos was forced to confront the fact that he was responsible for the deaths of many thousands of his own subjects, he relinquished the throne in favor of his son Fasil. After the abdication of Susenyos, missionaries and other Europeans were soon expelled altogether from Ethiopia. Ethiopia's unique faith was restored, not to be challenged again until the fall of the last Solomonic emperor, Haile Selassie, in the twentieth century.

### THE AGE OF THE PRINCES

Emperor Fasil inherited a deeply divided and demoralized state. Pummeled by outsiders and challenged from within, Abyssinia seemed to be a kingdom whose glories were far behind it. Fasil moved boldly, although in a way that would ultimately undermine the kingdom he sought to rebuild. Since 1270, when the Zagwe dynasty fell, Ethiopia had not had a permanent capital city, and, thinking to recapture the grandeur of Aksum, Fasil built a new capital further south at Gonder. He hoped, by restoring the trappings of power, to regain real power over church leaders and powerful landholders, now called princes.

For a while it worked. A period of relative calm ensued under a series of popular emperors, but by the time of Iyasu II, who ruled from 1730–1755, the princes of the various regions had begun to rebel. Fasil's creation of a centralized court at Gonder had backfired because emperors, expecting subordinates to come to them, no longer traveled much throughout the kingdom. This resulted in a gradual loss of control. Assassinations and other plots became common as real power shifted to the princes, who vied among themselves for appointment as the imperial *ras,* the equivalent of a grand duke. The period from the mid-1700s to the mid-1800s is referred to as *Zamana Masafent,* or the Age of the Princes. Though there were emperors, they were little more than figureheads, and the kingdom once again became little more than a collection of small states in which the *ras* was more revered and feared than the emperor himself.

## TEWODROS II AND THE RESURRECTION OF THE MONARCHY

The Age of the Princes ended when a remarkable person named Kas (or Kassa) Hayla, an Oromo, challenged and defeated rival princes and became the single leader of Ethiopia. In the words of Harold G. Marcus, "Kassa, one man, directed a battle against the *Zamana Masafent* and resoundingly won a united future for Ethiopia."[17] Afterward, in 1855, through a combination of diplomacy with clergy and princes and shows of force where needed, Kassa was crowned Emperor Tewodros II. Loyalty to him was shallow, however. When he took unpopular steps such as increasing taxes and confiscating what he considered to be surplus church lands, he lost what little support he had. According to Marcus, "Tewodros found himself the emperor of only that part of Ethiopia through which he and his large army marched, and no amount of pillaging and looting and terrorism seemed to make much of a difference."[18] He even at one point pillaged his own capital city of Gonder.

*The castle at Gonder was built during Emperor Fasil's reign.*

To ensure his hold on power, Tewodros invited an alliance with the British, which he presented as a chance to unite to eliminate the Muslim presence from the region. A series of miscommunications, misunderstandings, and acts of treachery culminated in Tewodros retreating to the mountains with several British hostages. In 1868, when the British army marched into Ethiopia to free them, Tewodros committed suicide rather than be humiliated by the consequences of his miscalculations.

## YOHANNES IV

Though Tewodros died a bitter and broken man, he nevertheless is remembered now as the one who restored a strong monarchy and ended a long period of decline for Ethiopia. However, it would take a while for his legacy to take hold. First, a prolonged struggle ensued between a Tigray leader, Yohannes IV, and a Shewa leader, Menelik II, both of whom declared themselves King of Kings, the name

*Crowned emperor in 1855, Tewodros II maintained power by terrorizing the people of Ethiopia.*

by which emperors were known in Ethiopia. After a few confrontations, the two leaders agreed to compromise, since both felt that to fight for power would ruin the country for both of them and also subject it to invasion. In 1876 Menelik became king of Shewa but in exchange had to agree to pay tribute and side militarily with Yohannes (who remained emperor of Ethiopia) against foreign powers.

A wary peace followed. Menelik never gave up his desire to rule Yohannes's land as well as his own. Over the next few years, each ruler tried to expand his power but avoided direct confrontation where possible. Eventually they decided to have their families intermarry, thus assuring a future victory for both sides when their heirs ruled a consolidated Ethiopia. Their uneasy alliance continued for another decade, ending only when Yohannes was killed in battle in 1889.

Menelik was now the undisputed emperor of all of Ethiopia. The old era of feudal warfare was at an end. Menelik was free to turn his attention to internal reforms and development and to shape the destiny of Ethiopia on the global stage in the early twentieth century. By the time Menelik died of old age in 1913, he had overseen the transition of Ethiopia into a new, more modern nation.

# 3

# STRUGGLING INTO THE MODERN ERA

While Yohannes IV was alive, Menelik II had been forced to play a secondary role in the history of the region. As king of Shewa, he had nowhere near the land or resources that Yohannes commanded, although he ruled over a sizable region of northeastern Ethiopia, including Tigray and Eritrea, and controlled access to the Red Sea. Pledged to mutual support against external enemies, the two men nevertheless continued to be wary of each other, and neither was above plotting against the other. Menelik was particularly adept at this, and indeed it is some of the moves he made as king of Shewa while Yohannes was still alive that would have the most far-reaching consequences for Ethiopia.

## ENTER THE ITALIANS

By 1889, when Menelik became emperor of Ethiopia, Africa was in the process of being carved up by European powers that wanted to establish colonies everywhere on the continent. On Ethiopia's borders, Great Britain was trying to strengthen its claims to the Sudan to the west and Kenya to the south, while France had colonized the tiny country of Djibouti to the east. Latecomers to colonialism, Italy saw that there was little left but Ethiopia to attempt to claim.

While Menelik was king of Shewa, he had viewed the Italians positively, thinking that with their arms and support he might be able to gain more territory and undercut Yohannes's power. With a shrewdness that would later characterize his long reign as emperor, he manipulated both sides, always to his own advantage. Menelik figured that if Italy moved to colonize Ethiopia, his best chance to gain more power was to be on friendly terms with the Italians.

Why not, he thought, let the Italians conquer Ethiopia for him and worry about controlling the Italians later?

Menelik underestimated the Italians, however. In May 1889 Menelik signed the Treaty of Wechale, which granted Italy the right to colonize what is today Eritrea, in exchange for an agreement to recognize that Ethiopia was an independent nation, and thus not to be interfered with by outsiders. Unknown to Menelik, the Italian language version was different from the one in Amharic, Menelik's language, in one very significant respect. Where the Amharic version said that Ethiopians *could* consult with the Italian government about their foreign affairs, the Italian version, which Menelik signed, said that they *must* consult Italy. Any nation that is forced to go through another nation to run its affairs is not independent, and thus, Menelik's signature appeared to have turned the entire region into an Italian protectorate.

The situation was aggravated when Italy showed the signed Italian version of the document to Great Britain's Queen Victoria and other European leaders, and they all, with the exception of France and Russia, accepted Italy's claim that it was now the legitimate colonial power in Ethiopia. When Menelik attempted to communicate with Queen Victoria, he was told that he could not correspond with her directly, but had to send messages through the Italian king. This and other humiliations turned Menelik against the Italians. On the other hand, Italy was also humiliated by the fact that it had bragged across all of Europe that it had a colony of its own, only to have its claim challenged and its trickery revealed. The situation, embarrassing for both sides, had to be resolved, and it appeared that warfare would be the only way.

*Emperor Menelik II, shown here with Empress Tahitou, fought to maintain Ethiopia's independence from Italy.*

## RINDERPEST

Rinderpest is a highly contagious, usually fatal viral disease affecting cattle and other hoofed animals. The disease was inadvertently brought to Africa by Italian troops in 1889, who brought infected cattle with them to use as a food supply. African cattle had no builtup resistance to the disease and died in huge numbers, as did other domesticated animals such as goats and pigs, and wild animals such as giraffes, antelope, and buffalo. Rinderpest swept south all the way to Cape Town, at the tip of South Africa, with disastrous consequences for hundreds of African ethnic groups.

For pastoralist people such as the Somali, life revolves around cattle and other herd animals. Social status is tied to owning animals, and the movements of people throughout the year are tied to the need to find grazing grounds. When the herds died, the cultures built around them were in chaos. There was nothing to eat, nothing to trade, and no way to cement relationships in cultures where giving or receiving livestock was an essential part of such things as marriage ceremonies and settlement of disputes. According to historian John Reader, in *Africa: A Biography of the Continent*, "Almost instantaneously, rinderpest swept away the wealth of tropical Africa," and the continuity of culture with it.

As if rinderpest was not enough, in the aftermath of the rinderpest epidemic, the tsetse fly, which causes the often fatal illness sleeping sickness in humans, was able to take hold in the new brush growth that was no longer being eaten by livestock. Human populations, already sick from starvation, were dealt another blow by sleeping sickness epidemics. All of this was taking place at a time when European colonial powers were trying to gain control of Africa. Historians point to the fact that many groups were too weakened to resist or felt that their only hope for survival lay in cooperation with those who offered food and medicine.

## ADWA

In 1895 Italy invaded Tigray from the base Menelik had permitted it to establish years before in Eritrea. Menelik mobilized a huge army of 100,000 soldiers from many regions of Ethiopia, fanning the fires of patriotism as he exhorted the troops to push the invaders off Ethiopian soil. The two forces met in the hills around the town of Adwa, where the Italian army was routed. Bloodshed was massive on both sides, but particularly devastating to the Italians, who lost 70 percent of their troops in this one battle. According to writer Philip Briggs, "The memory of the Battle of Adwa remains one of the proudest moments in Ethiopian history."[19] Indeed, it is one of the few times that an African army was able to fight off European armies determined to take African land.

After the Battle of Adwa, the Italian forces retreated back to Eritrea, and Menelik did not pursue them. Although it is possible that he could have pushed the Italians entirely off the continent, Menelik permitted them to remain in Eritrea, perhaps realizing that compromise was a better way to ensure his country's freedom in the long run. Menelik knew that there was an element of racism and simple miscalculation in the Italians' strategy. They had not expected to be beaten by a black army, and they had not even bothered to verify their maps, both critical elements in their defeat. Menelik knew that if the Italians felt shamed enough to try again with a larger, less cocky army to take the nation of Ethiopia by force, the outcome might be different. This face-saving that Menelik permitted the Italians would have important consequences in the future, long beyond his own lifetime, as Eritrea and Ethiopia developed increasingly separate identities.

*An illustration depicts soldiers of the Ethiopian cavalry and infantry in the war against Italy.*

## BUILDING THE ETHIOPIAN NATION

Whether it was Menelik's strategy or the shock of defeat that tamed the Italian's desire to colonize Ethiopia, no further attempt was made to gain a foothold beyond Eritrea until World War II, almost forty years later. Menelik's unquestioned status both at home and abroad as a strong emperor of a well-defended nation enabled him to turn his attention inward, and the rest of his reign is characterized by attempts at modernization. Urban Ethiopians had access to electricity, telephones, and public transportation for the first time under Menelik. A postal service and a national bank were established. The first public schools and hospitals were built, and the first vaccination program was undertaken, although these efforts only reached a small percentage of Ethiopia's population. Better roads were built, and a railroad connecting Menelik's new capital city of Addis Ababa with the coast in Djibouti was completed. This railroad ensured that Ethiopia would be a hub for trade between inland northeast Africa and the Red Sea coast and would thus make Addis Ababa the most important city in the region.

Despite such evidence, it is not clear that Menelik ever really understood what modernization meant. He was interested in having basic services at least in the cities, but he did not seem to grasp that modernization involved more than importing knowledge, skills, and technologies from abroad. Unlike some other modernizing nations in the same era, such as Japan, Menelik did not invest time into building industries and developing new skills among average citizens. He was content to introduce some rather superficial changes into a fundamentally unchanged society . Thus, though life for many had some modern touches, Ethiopia was not really advancing in terms of its ability to compete on world markets as a trading power. Still, Ethiopia seemed to be moving in a positive direction under Menelik II.

Menelik II died in 1913, but in the last few years of his reign he was increasingly incapacitated by syphilis, which affected his brain, and by a series of strokes. Infighting to determine who would succeed him was intense. The two figures to emerge from the power struggle were Menelik's daughter Zauditu and Ras Tafari Makonen, a nobleman from Harer. Because it was considered improper for a woman to rule, Zauditu was named empress, but real day-to-day power was exercised by Ras Tafari, who was also officially named as heir to Zauditu's throne. Sharing power did not work well, but the problem was resolved when Zauditu died, under somewhat suspicious circumstances, in 1930. Ras Tafari was crowned emperor late that year, at age thirty-eight, and took the name Haile Selassie, which means "Power of the Trinity" in Amharic.

## HAILE SELASSIE'S EARLY YEARS

Haile Selassie ruled Ethiopia for more than four decades. Typically seen wearing a military uniform covered with medals and decorations, Haile Selassie, with his distinctively sharp-featured face, became one of the most instantly recognizable world leaders, and he is undoubtedly one of the most important Africans of the twentieth century. For the first fourteen years of his reign, Haile Selassie concentrated on internal concerns, continuing some of the modernization projects undertaken by Menelik II and adding a few of his own, such as the establishment of newspapers, although they were forbidden to include anything critical of him.

Haile Selassie also was responsible for the country's first constitution, but it was not designed to give political power to the common people. For example, although there were to be two houses in the national assembly, typical of democracies around the world including the United States, Haile Selassie had the power to appoint all of the members. There were no elections. He stacked the assembly with Amhara and Tigray, causing resentment to grow among other groups. Just like Menelik before him, Haile Selassie had an old-fashioned sense of the absolute power of the monarchy and did not seem to understand the need to include the public in decision making, accept dissent and differences, and focus on the welfare of all citizens. Under Haile Selassie, the government continued to work primarily to meet the needs of only a small group of nobles and himself. The impoverished and difficult lives of most Ethiopians, particularly those who lived outside the major cities and towns, continued largely unchanged.

## WORLD WAR II

About the time Haile Selassie ascended the throne of Ethiopia, on the other side of the Mediterranean another leader was also on the rise. Unknown to Haile Selassie, Benito Mussolini, Italy's ruler, was contemplating renewing Italy's bid for a colony in Ethiopia. He hoped to impress other rising political leaders, such as Adolf Hitler of Germany and Joseph Stalin of the Soviet Union, with his leadership and vision, and to avenge Italy's defeat at Adwa almost forty years previously.

## THE RASTAFARIAN CONNECTION

The dreadlocks and highly rhythmic musical style of Jamaica's Bob Marley first brought a religious movement called Rastafarianism to the world's attention in the 1970s. However, many do not realize the Ethiopian link to this religion. It takes its name from Ras Tafari, Emperor Haile Selassie's name before his coronation.

Rastafarianism began in the 1930s in Jamaica in the period immediately following Haile Selassie's ascent to the throne. It was founded by Jamaican-born Marcus Garvey, who later immigrated to the United States and became the founder of a movement advocating that blacks escape racism by returning to Africa. Contemplating black people's struggle to overcome racism and fulfill their destiny as a people, Garvey came to believe that biblical phrases referring to the Messiah as a king who would arise in the east referred to Haile Selassie's crowning as emperor. Garvey advocated that Haile Selassie was indeed the true Messiah, the living God for the world's blacks.

Rastafarians believe there is one God, Jah, and that all races are equal in Jah's eyes. They believe the problems of the world are caused by white people's degeneration into evil because they have failed to respect that essential fact. There are approximately 700,000 Rastafarians around the world today, including approximately 60 percent of Jamaicans.

Ironically, Haile Selassie did not see himself the way Rastafarians do. In fact, when a group of Rastafarians attempted to visit him in Ethiopia, a palace guard sent them away, saying that their presence upset him. As a devout Christian he did not like the suggestion that anyone else other than Jesus was the Messiah.

*Marcus Garvey*

*Emperor Haile Selassie was responsible for the country's first constitution but retained the absolute power of the monarchy.*

   Still the official colonial power in Eritrea, Italy provoked Ethiopia into border skirmishes, then used one of these skirmishes as a pretext for a battle in the Ogaden at Welwel, near the Somali border. Italy complained to the League of Nations that Ethiopia had been the aggressor. Ethiopia countered that Italy had no right to be on Ethiopian land. Ethiopia was right, but a combination of factors, including unwillingness to provoke a wider war and a general pervasive racism caused the League to downplay the seriousness of issues brought to it by nonwhite leaders. The League of Nations ignored Selassie's appeal for support against Italy's incursions.
   When Mussolini saw that the nations of Europe were not going to support Ethiopia, he wasted no time invading from Italy's base in Eritrea. This time there was to be no repeat of the results at Adwa. The Italians marched across Ethiopia in 1935, using poison gas, bombs, and other drastic means to conquer the country. Haile Selassie tried to resist as long as

possible, but after a devastating Italian attack at the town of Maychew in 1936, he went into exile. Soon Ethiopia, Eritrea, and a portion of Somalia were renamed Italian East Africa. A month later, Haile Selassie delivered an impassioned appeal to the League of Nations, reminding them of Ethiopia's right to have its sovereignty respected on the same terms as any other nation. The League still did not act, and after the war, its shameful failure to do so was a key reason the organization disbanded.

Haile Selassie's decision to go into exile is still controversial. Some feel that he abandoned his country at a time of great need, and indeed this sentiment contributed to his decreasing popularity in the decades after World War II, when he was once again on the Ethiopian throne. As it was, Haile Selassie was able to claim that the monarchy had never been toppled because he was never removed as king, and as long as he was king there was still an Ethiopia. His exile effectively made the point that invaders were illegitimately in his country, and his ceaseless efforts to keep Ethiopia's troubles in the international spotlight are one of his finest accomplishments as emperor.

When World War II broke out, Ethiopia suddenly found that western powers were more willing to support it. Italy was one of the Axis powers, siding with Germany. Great Britain was on the other side, part of the Allied forces. The war was fought in many locations around the world, including North Africa. Great Britain, which had vital economic interests in the Sudan and Kenya, wanted to push Italy out of Ethiopia and thus keep the Sudanese and Kenyan borders safe and the Red Sea open for trade and for the movement of Allied troops. A combined army of British and Ethiopian soldiers (who had been training over the border in the Sudan and Kenya) joined with Ethiopian guerrilla fighters called *arbagna* who had stayed behind in occupied Ethiopia, and together they were able to push the Italians out of the country by 1941. Haile Selassie returned, and the Italian occupation was over. A few years later, in 1945, World War II ended, and Selassie emerged on the world stage as one of the war's great figures and moral leaders—a man who in the face of great adversity never lost his dignity and never gave up on winning back his country.

## ETHIOPIA AFTER THE WAR

The Italian occupation, though it lasted only five years, had some major long-term political and economic effects on the country. Haile Selassie, who expected simply to return to his old, and still largely feudal way of ruling, was not well equipped to deal with these changes. Eventually, though it took several decades, his shortsightedness would lead to his downfall and the end of the Solomonic monarchy in Ethiopia.

The Italian occupation had a big effect on the country because it had been a particularly brutal one. For example, in 1937 an attempt was made on the life of the viceroy, the person the Italians appointed to serve as the official leader of Ethiopia. In vengeance, Italian troops ran wild through the streets of Addis Ababa, burning and looting, and killing as many as thirty thousand citizens through such brutal methods as disembowelment and decapitation. The nobility and the country's most educated citizens were particular targets for suppression because they were perceived (with good

*Italian soldiers march toward Addis Ababa on March 3, 1936. The invasion by Italy drove Haile Selassie into exile.*

reason) as the leaders of the growing resistance movement. In fact, few members of Ethiopia's elite survived the occupation. The destruction of the nobility, which had formed an important part of the country's political structure, and the overall loss of population—especially the intellectuals—made political and economic recovery more difficult.

Additionally, the Italians had moved quickly during the occupation to remake Ethiopia into a economically valuable colony. They substantially enlarged the network of paved roads, especially through the difficult terrain of the mountain plateaus, to improve commerce. The Italians also began the process of replacing small subsistence farms with what they hoped would be successful large plantations. The net effect was that subsistence farming was dealt a huge blow, but nothing worked in its place. When they left, the Italians abandoned lands they had taken from peasants but had never turned into operational farms.

## THE FALL OF HAILE SELASSIE

Across Africa, the decade following the end of World War II was a time of unrest and growing efforts to overthrow colonial governments and reclaim Africa for indigenous Africans. Ethiopia's situation was unusual in that there was no outsider to remove, but in many respects Haile Selassie represented at least some of the same perceived evils. Though he would continue to rule until 1974, it was clear that he had no real interest in a truly democratic Ethiopia and saw no reason that he should not continue to run the country as if it were his own personal property. Though he was still revered as the heir to a long line of Solomonic rulers, what he symbolized was no longer acceptable to a growing number of Ethiopians.

Haile Selassie's Ethiopia was a favored target for western aid. He played on his country's Christian heritage as a common bond with the west, and his declared anticommunism made his country one of the most strategic points in the world during the cold war. The United States in particular was so eager to stay on friendly terms with Ethiopia that it was willing to go along with anything Haile Selassie wanted. Haile Selassie became more and more brutal in his suppression of dissent and became increasingly dictatorial in all aspects of his rule. When the first of a series of years of drought killed a quarter of a million people in Tigray in 1973, rather than acknowledge the legitimacy of the peasants' calls for land reform, Haile Selassie put down their protests by force. After this point such a wide range of people in Ethiopia were dissatisfied with Haile Selassie that they were able to mount an insurrection that led to his arrest and removal in September 1974. As Philip Briggs puts it, "Three thousand years of Solomonic rule ended with an octogenarian emperor being driven unceremoniously from his palace in a Volkswagen Beetle."[20]

## THE *DERG*

Haile Selassie's downfall came about because such a wide range of people were dissatisfied with his leadership. People advocating greater autonomy for Oromo, Tigray, and Eritrea had joined with ideological groups ranging from communists to democrats to bring about change. However, once the objective of Haile Selassie's removal was achieved, there was no agreement about what to do next. Those who had participated in toppling the monarchy soon found that the future of Ethiopia was not going to be decided by civilized discussion and compromise but by force. Whether the country would be democratic or communist, whether it would stay intact or splinter into small ethnic states, or whether something altogether different would happen was clearly going to depend on who was most willing and able to use fear and violence to gain the upper hand.

The repression Ethiopia would suffer was quickly set in motion by the Coordinating Committee of the Armed Forces, which was generally referred to simply as the *Derg* (or "committee" in Amharic). Using the slogan "Ethiopia Tikdem," or "Ethiopia First," they proclaimed that the only way to ensure order and prosperity, at least in the short run while basic questions about Ethiopia's future were worked out, was to have the military rule the country. The first *Derg* leader to serve as head of state after Haile Selassie's departure was Aman Mikhail Andom, an Eritrean general who favored democratic reforms and substantial autonomy for Eritrea and other regions. However, Aman's views were not shared by many of the *Derg's* other leaders. Frustrated, Aman began to conspire against them, but the plot was revealed through a tap on his phone, and he was killed on *Derg* orders when he resisted arrest as a traitor.

*Haile Selassie is
pictured in his palace
office in Addis Ababa.
In 1974 Ethiopians
became dissatisfied
with his leadership and
removed him from
office.*

In the aftermath of Aman's death, the subsequent execution of fifty-nine men, including generals, royalty and cabinet members, "shocked the nation and the world," writes historian Harold G. Marcus. "The event revealed that a ruthless military regime controlled Ethiopia, and . . . tempered with blood, it would follow its own path."[21] Realizing that it needed to move quickly to establish a clear direction for the country, the *Derg* leadership proclaimed that from henceforth Ethiopia would develop along socialist lines. What this meant in essence was that people who previously had owned a great deal of property had to give it up so that people who had less or none at all could have a fairer share. Urban neighborhoods and farming communities were to be run by PAs, or peasant associations, which would decide how land was to be divided and oversee community life in general. The *Derg* also took a position against autonomy for Eritrea, angering the Eritrean supporters of the coup against Haile Selassie.

## ERITREAN INDEPENDENCE

When the Italians were defeated in World War II, within months of Haile Selassie's triumphant return to Ethiopia, the United Nations revoked Italy's claim to a colony in Eritrea. Poor and underdeveloped, Eritrea did not seem ready to sustain itself economically. Concerned that a weak Eritrea might be vulnerable to a communist takeover, which would threaten access to the Red Sea and trade through the Suez Canal, the United States and other western powers, acting through the United Nations, promoted the idea of Eritrea becoming part of Ethiopia again. Eritreans, who had their own distinct regional culture they wanted to protect, were unwilling simply to be just another part of Ethiopia. Therefore, in 1953, the citizenry voted to become an autonomous territory within Ethiopia, meaning that their country would retain significant rights to self-government although not be fully independent. By the 1960s, however, Haile Selassie was no longer respecting Eritrea's autonomy, acting as if it was in every way simply another part of Ethiopia. Unhappy Eritreans formed the Eritrean People's Liberation Front (EPLF) and began a campaign of civil disobedience and terrorism to push for full independence.

By 1975 Ethiopia and Eritrea were engaged in a full-scale civil war in cities and in countryside, a war that raged for another ten years, taking thousands of lives, devastating the economy, and causing mass homelessness and starvation. By 1991, the EPLF had captured key cities and was able to establish a provisional government separate from Ethiopia. After the fall of Mengistu in 1991, there was little Ethiopia could do to keep the inevitable from happening. In a special referendum in 1993, over 99 percent of Eritreans voted for independence, and later that year, Eritreans elected their first president, Issayas Afewerki.

In 1999 hostilities regarding the proper border between the two countries resumed. Eritrean troops invaded along the border, and casualties have been heavy on both sides. Many feel that Eritrea is taking advantage of Ethiopia's drought and seeking to expand its territory while Ethiopia is distracted by other concerns. Ethiopia is determined not to let any territory go, especially by means it considers underhanded. Although a cease-fire was successfully negotiated in mid-2000, the issues remain unresolved and it is unlikely that peace has been permanently achieved.

Though strong stances often give the impression that there is strong leadership behind them, in Ethiopia this was not really the case. *Derg* leaders, including Mengistu Haile Mariam, who became the undisputed leader of Ethiopia in 1977, rarely had any deep, heartfelt commitment to any political philosophy and did not really understand how to go about creating a socialist state. The *Derg* encouraged flag waving, slogans, and marches to make it appear as if there were a glorious revolution going on in Ethiopia, but in fact, they had no viable plan for building the country along socialist lines. Ironically, the failure of communism in Eastern Europe and the Soviet Union was beginning to be apparent just at the time Mengistu and the *Derg* were trying to jump on board.

## THE MENGISTU ERA

There was still no real consensus about such things as what kind of government Ethiopia should have and where its borders should be drawn. The only real consensus was a grim one: In the words of Philip Briggs, "Those who opposed [Mengistu] didn't do so for long."[22] In fact, Mengistu came to be head of state through trumped up evidence he used to justify arresting and executing his last powerful opponent, General Tafari Bente, in 1977. Once in office, Mengistu declared a "Red Terror," designed to sweep the country clean of those who opposed him, under the guise of ridding the country of those whose views and actions stood in the way of the socialist revolution. According to Harold G. Marcus, "Unspeakable horrors were perpetrated on a largely defenseless civilian population . . . killing or forcing into exile thousands of Ethiopia's best-educated and idealistic young people."[23] Mengistu was so ruthless that opposition seemed to vanish, especially after such horrifying events as the murder of five hundred students one night in May 1978. Dead bodies in the streets became part of the scenery during those dark days.

Mengistu's power was based on his ability to command the military to do his bidding, not on any real support among the people. The country was in open revolt even before he took power, because the "revolution" was decreeing changes in the way people lived without any real plan or resources to make the changes work. For example, Ethiopians were forced to relocate to villages along main roads, supposedly to make government services easier to provide, and were pressured to work as part of farming collectives rather than individually, as was the tradition. Both of these moves were hated. The PAs came to be viewed as means to brainwash people and collect taxes, rather than as a way to give people more power. Furthermore, regions like Eritrea were taking advantage of the chaos and dissatisfaction to strengthen their own drives for independence.

## AFTER MENGISTU

All Mengistu really could do was put on a show to make Ethiopia look like a success story and kill anyone who undercut this effort. By the mid-1980s, despite the danger involved, opposition to him was growing. Several factors, including the general population's anger at Mengistu's handling of severe famines and the strength of a number of ethnic movements advocating secession from Ethiopia, made Mengistu's downfall inevitable. What finally broke his regime was the collapse of communism, which put an end to Mengistu's most important source of foreign aid. When rebel troops appeared poised to capture Addis Ababa in May 1991, Mengistu Haile Mariam, without a word even to his closest advisers, escaped to Zimbabwe, where he lives today.

*Mengistu Haile Mariam ruled Ethiopia from 1977 to 1991. His "Red Terror" campaign sought to eliminate anyone who opposed him.*

The Mengistu era was at an end, but Ethiopia's future was still far from certain. None of the issues so important after the fall of Haile Selassie—how to ensure national unity but still respect ethnic differences, what kind of government to have, how to ensure people's basic needs are met, how to

# THE POLITICS OF FAMINE

In 1984, while Mengistu was spending lavishly on a celebration of the tenth anniversary of the self-styled "glorious revolution" that toppled Haile Selassie, one-sixth of the total population of the country he led was in danger of dying of starvation, and ten thousand people per week were already dying in the hardest-hit province, Welo. The rains first failed to come in summer 1983, then again in winter 1984, giving Mengistu plenty of time to heed the warnings that the subsequent crop failures would lead to starvation, mass death, and social disruption. Mengistu refused to acknowledge the famine, and would not ask for international aid. According to Harold G. Marcus, in *A History of Ethiopia,* "The government was unwilling to divert resources, money, and attention away from the . . . celebrations; and it certainly was not going to admit the existence of a famine worse than the one that had shattered Haile Selassie's reign." When the international guests (mostly communist leaders) left Ethiopia, Mengistu begrudgingly acknowledged the problem and allowed television and other journalists to visit the hardest hit sites. International relief efforts, including the one organized by Irish rock musician Bob Geldof, which produced the hit song "We Are the World," soon brought the immediate problem under control.

As part of the "politics of famine," Mengistu began using his power to block delivery of grain to areas he considered hostile to him, most notably Tigray and Eritrea. Innocent people starved to death while grain sat undelivered. However, the

politics of famine did not end with Mengistu. In late 1999 and early 2000, huge shipments of grain and other humanitarian aid remained undeliverable when tensions between now independent Eritrea and Ethiopia flared over which ports would be used to unload the ships delivering the aid.

*An Ethiopian refugee carries a starving boy. In 1984, many Ethiopians starved because aid could not reach them.*

become more self-sufficient, and how to become an economic and political force in the modern world—had been addressed by Mengistu. In fact, many of those who asked such questions in good faith were killed or exiled. Now, after Mengistu, the questions needed to be asked anew, and people needed to rebuild their confidence in their government.

Though Ethiopia still is one of the poorest and most economically backward countries in the world, it appears to be trying to address these pressing problems. Its new leaders, President Negasso Gidada and Prime Minister Meles Zenawi, in power since 1995, so far have managed to avoid the repressiveness of the past, have overseen the adoption of a legitimate constitution, and have pledged to make the country a multiparty democracy. But Ethiopia's problems are bigger than any two men can solve with good intentions. It will take a concerted effort by all Ethiopians, well thought out programs by the government, and international assistance based on genuine concern rather than political advantage, to make Ethiopia the vibrant international power and smoothly functioning culture it was under the early Solomonic rulers at Aksum several thousand years ago.

# 4

# DAILY LIFE IN ETHIOPIA

Ethiopia is a land of tremendous diversity. This diversity goes far beyond ethnicity, although there are approximately seventy different ethnic-based languages in the country. Ethiopia's diversity is also illustrated by its many religious faiths. Beyond Islam and Christianity, there are still pockets of Falasha, who practice a variety of Judaism, and practitioners of traditional African religions. Its diversity is also illustrated by the geography of the country, which has a profound effect on residents, ranging from the fierce Afar who live in the stiflingly hot and dry Danakil Depression in the northeast; to the Somali, who wander the deserts of the southeast; to the elite Amhara on the western plateau.

It might seem at first glance, therefore, that it would be difficult to describe typical Ethiopian life because customs inevitably will vary from group to group depending on religion, tradition, and the specific challenges of different physical environments. However, in Ethiopia, one simple fact cuts through many of these differences: The country is 90 percent rural, comprised primarily of tiny, isolated farming communities on the plateaus and small, nomadic communities in the lowlands, in both of which survival is a daily struggle.

The remaining 10 percent of the population almost all live in the capital, Addis Ababa, the only large city in the country. The next largest communities, though they are called cities, would be considered medium-sized towns in the United States, with populations about seventy thousand. Thus, even in cities such as Dire Dawa, people generally live in ways more like those of a typical farming community than an urban center. Because of this fact, although the details of daily life might vary somewhat by religion, ethnic traditions, size of community, or location, most Ethiopians live in many respects very similar lives.

## THE COMMUNITIES OF RURAL ETHIOPIA

For centuries the average Ethiopian lived in a community too small even to be called a village. In fact, during the *Derg*, a program to pull rural Ethiopians into larger communities was called "villagization." The typical and traditional rural farming community was—and in many parts of Ethiopia still is—comprised of fewer than half a dozen huts, each the dwelling of usually only one family, consisting of a husband and wife and their children, and perhaps an elderly relative or two. Today, as in the past, the small clusters of huts serve primarily as an extra measure of protection against wild animals rather than as a way of pooling labor between families. In fact, this element of protection is so essential that the family cows, chickens, or goats are usually brought inside for the night.

*Gochos (pictured) are woven from young saplings and then covered with thatched grass.*

Housing in rural Ethiopia varies by ethnic group, but homes generally tend to be one room, made from materials at hand. Sometimes, as in the case of a *gocho,* a common style of round

## THE SPIRIT WORLD

According to scholars for the Library of Congress, reporting in *Ethiopia: A Country Guide,* "Belief in the existence of active spirits—many malevolent, some benevolent—is widespread among Ethiopians, whether Christian, Muslim, or pagan." Spirits are of several types. *Zar* have definite personalities, male or female, and are able to prevent trouble if they wish to help an individual. Thus, believers will try to be friendly and kind to any *zar* they feel is interested in them. *Adbar* spirits are similarly helpful, but they do not intervene on behalf of individuals. They instead belong to the community. Female *adbars* specialize in protection from such things as disease and poverty, whereas male *adbars* prevent fights and wars and help in bringing about good harvests.

A third category of myths is associated with *buda,* best translated as the "evil eye." People wear special charms to ward off *buda* and also offer special prayers. Wizards can also be consulted to determine why misfortune has occurred and suggest ways to remove the influence of *buda.*

house, the walls are woven from young sapling trees and the roof is covered with thatched grass. Some houses have tin roofs and others are built from stone, but they all have in common their small size and, usually, one-room structure. Inside the houses, furniture is sparse. People sleep on animal skin rugs or on wooden cots. Three-legged stools and a *masob,* a table woven from straw, complete the furnishings. Nomadic dwellings are similarly basic, often no more than woven grass mats or animal skins flung over frames made of bent branches, constructed in a way that makes them easy to take down and transport by camel across the arid terrain.

Whatever the style of house, in most rural Ethiopian communities, the family inside is entirely responsible for meeting its own needs. In this respect, Ethiopia is unlike some other parts of Africa which have a strong tradition of communal effort in such matters as child rearing and cooking. In Ethiopia, meals are generally prepared by each family rather than collectively, and children are considered to be the responsibility of their parents. Small plots of land belong to particular families, who plow, plant, and harvest crops themselves. This lifestyle of subsistence farming, in which a barely adequate food supply is eked out each year by the intense labor of individual families, was undercut in recent years by natural and political events such as drought, famine, and specific attempts by the *Derg* to bring Ethiopians into larger villages and onto huge, state-run farms. However, the small subsistence farm remains the norm today.

Some of the social upheavals of the present day are felt by some experts to be a result of tearing Ethiopians away from their traditional way of life, but in fact, much about life in these larger villages remains in many respects unchanged from past centuries. Even the communities created by "villagization" are extremely small and isolated, consisting of from several dozen to several hundred huts linked to other villages by dirt roads. Thus, though typical rural Ethiopians today may travel a little farther from home and live in a slightly larger community, they conduct their daily lives much as the generations have before them.

## FOOD AND DRINK

One of the ways that life in rural Ethiopia never seems to change is that it constantly revolves around getting enough to eat. More than three-quarters of Ethiopians go hungry on a typical day. In cultures where food is hard to come by, distinctions between work and home life, and between the lives of children and adults, become very blurred because the waking hours of everyone in the family are tied in one way or another to getting, preparing, and eating whatever food is available.

Likewise, meeting the basic need for water is an ongoing concern. Villages in rural Ethiopia usually have one central source of water—a well, spring, river, or lake. Each family must take buckets to the water source to bring back what it needs. Running water in homes is unheard of, and the water carried back must suffice for washing and food preparation. Washing is an important ritual, and as long as adequate water is available, family members will begin the day by splashing a small amount of water on their face and hands to clean up before breakfast. In nomadic communities, where water is even more treasured, such rituals are usually not found.

Water brought back in the morning is poured over coffee beans, which have been roasted over an open fire and ground only minutes before. Ethiopians treat drinking coffee as a ceremony and usually follow a special procedure to prepare and serve it. Only children drink milk, which may come from cows, camels, or goats. Everyone else drinks coffee in the morning, flavored with salt, honey, or sugar. This emphasis on coffee should not come as much of a surprise because coffee is indigenous to Ethiopia and has expanded to other parts of the world from this source. Later in the day, *talla,* a beer made from barley is a popular beverage. It is only slightly alcoholic, and is considered suitable for both adults and children. An Ethiopian honey wine called *tej* is also frequently consumed, but overall Ethiopians do not drink much alcohol.

The basic diet of rural Ethiopians revolves around *injera,* which resembles a large sourdough pancake, and is, according to the Lonely Planet on-line guide, "phenomenally bouncy."[24] *Injera* is usually made of teff, the most popular grain in Ethiopia, which is either ground between stones or pounded into a flour. The grain generally comes from the most recent harvest of the family farm, although families try to maintain a surplus in case of drought. Grinding may be done by individual housewives in the quantity needed by their family for a few days, or in larger villages grain may be taken to a mill for grinding. *Injera* can also be made from other grains such as wheat, barley, or corn, if they are available, but teff is by far the most common.

*Injera* is used to scoop up whatever other food is available. This may include the popular spicy stew known as *wat,*

*Women at a communal water well fill their jugs to carry back to their communities.*

which is usually made of vegetables such as onions, peppers, and cabbage grown in the family garden, but may contain chicken or beef on special occasions. Because Ethiopian Christianity, Islam, and Judaism all prohibit eating pork, this meat is rarely found in Ethiopia. Nomadic Ethiopians rarely slaughter the animals on which their lives depend. Rather, they subsist on a mixture of animal blood, obtained by cutting into veins on the animal's neck, and milk, which they supplement with whatever other food they can find.

## FAMILY ROLES IN RURAL ETHIOPIA

In rural Ethiopian communities, everyone, with the exception of very small children, has a role to play in his or her family's survival. Young children are responsible by the age of three for simple tasks such as putting the cow and chickens outside in the morning and shooing baboons, birds, and other animals out of the garden and fields. Young children also perform simple tasks such as collecting firewood and running errands. Once children are about eight years old they start performing tasks considered suitable to their gender. For example, young boys begin learning from their fathers how to plow the land with ox-drawn wooden plows and how to tend crops. They may also be assigned to guard cows and other livestock that are put out to pasture. Nomadic boys learn how to keep track of and manage herds.

Injera, *the staple food of rural Ethiopians, resembles a large sourdough pancake.*

Young girls from the age of eight are responsible for helping with the cooking and are taught how to select goods and bargain for them at the market. They learn how to do a wide range of women's tasks such as selecting, drying, and pounding the spices needed for *wat* and other dishes. By caring for the young children in the household, girls learn parenting skills they will need when they marry, usually around the age of fifteen or sixteen.

## RURAL SCHOOLING

With such a delineation of labor, rural Ethiopian families are able, at least in good rainfall years, to get their needs met without outside assistance. However, because every family member has an important role to play, there is often no time to go to school. As a result, the literacy rate of Ethiopians is very low. Approximately 90 percent of the population could not read or write at the time the *Derg* took power, and though improving literacy was one of its goals, it had only modest success. Today the literacy rate is approximately 35 percent, with males almost twice as likely to know how to read as females.

In rural areas, literacy is far lower than in Addis Ababa, both among people living in settled villages and in those nomadic groups. The problem is aggravated by the fact that even if a child could be spared from household responsibilities, approximately three-quarters of rural Ethiopians live nowhere near a school. Those who do are often educated by people who are not well schooled themselves, are poorly paid, and are not widely respected in the community. Additionally, the schools are usually little more than huts with mud benches, where teachers must carry on without adequate supplies of books, writing implements, and other basic supplies. It is

## TELLING TIME IN ETHIOPIA

Not only does Ethiopia use a different alphabet than any other country, it has a unique way of telling time and dividing the year as well. The Ethiopian day begins at sunrise, which does not vary much throughout the year because Ethiopia is close to the equator. Therefore to Ethiopians what we would call 7 A.M. is one o'clock. Time is told in twelve, hour increments, just as in the west, so 7 P.M. is one o'clock again.

The Ethiopian calendar is divided into twelve months of thirty days each, followed by a thirteenth month of five days (or six in leap year). The new year begins on September 11, which to Ethiopians is called Meskerem 1.

This unique way of structuring time is evidence of how separately Ethiopian culture evolved from other cultures. Ethiopians doing business with the west have adjusted to the European calendar and system of telling time, but the rest of Ethiopia continues to follow tradition.

hardly a surprise that it has been difficult to convince rural Ethiopians to send their children to school.

## RELIGIOUS CELEBRATIONS

Although daily life is in many respects the same all over Ethiopia in that it is a daily struggle to survive, and few opportunities exist for improving one's life, the diversity of Ethiopia can be clearly seen in the customs of the various religions. Especially in rural areas, these celebrations remain intense expressions of faith. The most important holiday for Christians, Timkat, which celebrates the baptism of Jesus, falls on January 19, two weeks after the Ethiopian Christmas (Ganna). The Ethiopian New Year, Enkutatash, considered a religious festival to Christians, is celebrated on September 11, when the rainy season is officially over. According to the Lonely Planet on-line guide, "Enkutatash is a festival, with [young people] dancing in the streets, handing out flowers and miniature paintings, bonfires and plenty of singing and dancing."[25] It is quickly followed by another very important holiday, Maskal, on September 27, which celebrates the legend of the finding of the cross on which Jesus was crucified. Kullubi is celebrated on December 28 and acknowledges St. Gabriel, considered to be a miracle worker and protector. It is common for large groups of pilgrims to walk long distances to celebrate holidays in sacred cities such as Lalibela, and according to photographer and author Kazuyoshi Nomachi, "After participating . . . many must trek as long as a fortnight to reach home."[26]

Muslims also have a number of special holidays, generally the same ones as fellow believers all over the world. The most important is Ramadan, a month during which all devout Muslims are expected to refrain from food and drink during all daylight hours as a means of refocusing on their faith. In Ethiopia, where many Muslims live in the searing heat of the desert, accommodations must be made to preserve the health of the community, and refraining from water during the day is not considered necessary to prove one's devotion to Allah. The small remaining communities of Falasha, who today live mostly in Gonder, observe Passover and Rosh Hashanah along with fellow Jews all over the world, but because they broke from the mainstream Jewish faith very early, they do not celebrate holidays added later, such as the spring festival of Purim.

In Ethiopia there are also several holidays celebrated regardless of religion. Some of these are associated with political events, and others are associated with seasons of the year. The

## TIMKAT

Over two hundred days a year have special celebrations associated with them in the Ethiopian Christian community. However, Timkat, celebrated on January 19, is considered the most important religious holiday of the year. It is considered the equivalent of the western Christian festival of the Epiphany, which in Ethiopia is associated with the baptism of Jesus. Preparations for Timkat begin well in advance of the holiday. Children get new clothes and small gifts, and special care is taken to ensure that all *shammas* are bright white. Beer is brewed, bread is baked, and a lamb is slaughtered for a special lamb stew to be eaten after the ceremonies.

Celebrations are held across Ethiopia to commemorate Timkat. The festivities include parades, speeches, and street parties in Addis Ababa, a highlight of which is the appearance of the *Abun,* head of the Ethiopian Orthodox Church, in splendid ceremonial robes. However, in the Ethiopian countryside the holiday is still celebrated much as it has been for hundreds of years. Timkat officially begins the evening before the celebrations, when priests clad in brightly striped and embroidered gowns and carrying ornately jeweled and embroidered umbrellas cover with bright silks a box called a *tabot,* symbolizing the Ark of the Covenant. They take the *tabot* from the church and proceed with it to a river, pool, or other water source. There it is left, carefully guarded, for the night. In the

morning the water is blessed, and baptisms take place. People bathe in the newly sanctified water and fling handfuls to those unable to get to the water's edge. Later, *debteras* lead a traditional line dance back to the church, where the *tabot* is returned to its place and the feast begins.

*An Ethiopian deacon carries a* tabot *during a Timkat festival.*

most prominent example of the former is celebrated on March 2 to commemorate Menelik's victory over the Italian army at Adwa in 1890. An example of the latter is Buhe, celebrated in August, which has evolved into a children's holiday similar in some respects to Halloween in that children go house to house singing for offerings of bread. The celebration ends with a noisy celebration around a huge bonfire.

## CELEBRATING LIFE'S PASSAGES

In Ethiopia, as everywhere in the world, important celebrations are often family affairs. Many deeply meaningful and often elaborate celebrations are associated with the important events in life. Birth, puberty, marriage, and death in particular are marked by community celebrations that vary from region to region and among ethnic and religious groups.

For example, in Ethiopian Christian homes, children are often not given names for several weeks. This is in part due to the high infant mortality rate, which makes parents understandably cautious about becoming too closely bonded with a newborn, and in part because, according to the U.S. Department of State post report on Ethiopia, "Ethiopian custom is to name persons to emphasize their individuality."[27] Boys are baptized and named forty days after birth, but girls wait eighty days. Babies are then given meaningful names, often reflecting the hardships of life, such as Attalel ("may he/she trick death"), Biyadgillign ("I hope he grows up for me"), or Sintayyehu ("I have seen so very much"). Other popular names such as Tesfaye ("my hope"), Nur Addis ("new life"), or Allefnew ("we have made it through hard times"), celebrate the miracle of the new child's existence. Sometimes the children also have a secret baptismal name known only within the family. Baptisms are important events celebrated with as elaborate a feast as the parents can afford.

Marriage celebrations vary so widely across Ethiopia that few generalizations seem valid except that marriage is inevitably accompanied by elaborate and often lengthy rituals. One of the first steps usually involves negotiations by the prospective bride and groom's families. Usually the groom's family compensates the bride's family for taking someone important away from them. This payment is called bridewealth. In the event of divorce, which is considered acceptable if a marriage is not working well, it is often expected that the bridewealth will be returned.

Engagement ceremonies and the wedding itself are often accompanied by specific rituals, such as face painting or parades. Usually there is a feast associated with the wedding itself, after which the bride and groom go on the equivalent of a honeymoon, which often consists of a stay in a private tent or hut for a week or so. Friends and family may bring food and provide entertainment, but the couple is expected to stay inside until the honeymoon is over. Often weddings are very stressful times for the bride, because among many Ethiopian groups female circumcision is still practiced either at puberty or shortly before the wedding, and it makes consummating the marriage, as well as subsequent childbirth painful, difficult, and occasionally even life threatening.

Customs for handling death vary widely by faith and ethnic group. Funerals often have two distinct parts, *merdo*, which is the ceremony surrounding the announcement of the death, and *legso*, which is the ritual of mourning. Burials themselves are handled differently from group to group. For example the Surma of southern Ethiopia bury their dead in a seated position, after placing their possessions in the grave with them. Before the grave is sealed with earth, a series of

## THE *SHAMMA*

No other article of clothing is so closely associated with Ethiopia as the *shamma*. The *shamma* is a large, approximately five-by-ten-foot rectangle of lightweight white cotton cloth, around which a brightly colored border has usually been embroidered. Worn by men and women alike, especially among the Tigray and Amhara, today it is more commonly worn by women on a daily basis and by men only on ceremonial occasions. The *shamma* is worn draped loosely over the shoulders and arms, and may be pulled up over the head to form a hood. Generally women wear a lightweight white dress called a *k'amis* underneath the *shamma*, and men wear a white shirt and trousers. The *shamma* is an ideal garment to provide some protection from the sun yet not overheat the wearer. It also provides some wind resistance in higher mountain regions. Thus, although western dress is common in cities, particularly in business settings, the *shamma* has continued to be a standard item of apparel across Ethiopia.

chants tells the story of the dead person's life. Often to ensure proper funeral celebrations, villages will set up funds to which members contribute regularly. These funds are used for whatever funerals are needed during the year. In fact, in many Ethiopian cultures, funerals are considered by far the most important celebrations, outweighing baptisms and weddings.

*In certain Ethiopian communities, funerals are more important celebrations than baptisms or weddings.*

## LIFE IN ADDIS ABABA

Although many of the traditions of the countryside are practiced in the capital city as well, life there is in many respects different. Addis Ababa has grown in the century since its founding into a large city of approximately 3 million people. This growth has been largely unplanned, and as a result the city seems rather disorganized and chaotic. Most streets are not signposted, for example, and the lack of an overall zoning plan has resulted in neighborhoods where crowded and squalid mud huts stand side by side with modern apartment buildings. Because for many residents the only transportation is their feet, neighborhoods tend to be self-sufficient and close knit, giving some parts of Addis Ababa the flavor of rural villages.

Though streets and roads are in poor condition overall, they are crowded with cars. Adding to the chaos of Addis Ababa is the general disregard motorists and pedestrians alike have for laws of basic safety. In fact, according to the U.S. government post report, no means of transportation—private car, cab, or bus—is really safe.

## DEBTERAS

In Ethiopia, where so many people are deeply devout, becoming a priest is not always so much a result of feeling a special vocation but more a practical career decision. For example, it is common for the blind to become monks because the monasteries provide a more accommodating lifestyle than the outside world. Though there are a number of different kinds of clergy and a hierarchy within the church, for practical purposes, the clergy can be divided into two categories, *kahinat* and *debteras*. The *kahinat* includes all priests, apprentice priests called deacons, and some monks. *Debteras* are sometimes former *kahinat* who for some reason have lost their ordination. This might occur as a result of a change in their marital status, for example. Priests can be either married or celibate, but this is a decision they must commit to before they are ordained. If they violate whichever path they have taken, they are considered ritually impure and can no longer be priests.

More often *debteras* are individuals who decided not to be part of the *kahinat* in the first place. For a poor Ethiopian boy of above average intelligence, becoming a *debtera* may be very appealing because *debteras* spend most of their time studying, learning special skills, and teaching others. According to researchers of the Library of Congress, in *Ethiopia: A Country Study*, "*debteras* act as choristers, poets, herbalists, astrologers, fortune-tellers, and scribes." It may take as long as twenty years for a *debtera* to learn all of the songs, dances, poetry, literature, and religious philosophy he is supposed to know. The *debteras* are widely respected religious figures across Ethiopia and they are responsible for ensuring that ceremonies, such as those associated with Timkat, Maskal, and other holidays, are performed correctly.

The main streets are paved, but many side streets are rocky, and, in the rainy season, very muddy. All streets suffer from neglect and large pot holes. Traffic is impaired not only by road conditions, but also by unruly drivers, animals, pedestrians walking on the roadway, and very poor street lighting. . . . Road accidents in Addis Ababa are very high, fatalities frequent, and medical care very poor.[28]

The chaos of the streets is mirrored in the bustling activity of the city center. Blue and white taxis jostle to get by donkeys laden with loads of straw and street vendors pushing their carts. Homeless children and deformed and disabled people beg for change. Lining the streets of the central market district are makeshift shops and factories where people sew clothes, grind spices, and hawk produce and souvenirs. The central business district, clustered around a former open air parade ground called Revolution Square, is characterized by high-rise buildings constructed mostly in the 1960s and showing obvious signs of wear. City hall and Addis Ababa University are both in this area and attract not only students and businessmen but the usual assortment of beggars and thieves, as well as merchants hoping to make a little money selling beverages or something quick to eat.

Addis Ababa is a difficult place to live, but many Ethiopians come to the city each year because it offers opportunities to get ahead that are lacking in their small villages. Most of the country's factories are located in the capital city, producing such things as textiles, shoes and clothing, plastics, and chemical products. Thus, opportunities for employment are presumed to be greater. Food supplies are more reliable as well, and there are far better opportunities to get a basic education. However, Addis Ababa is not equipped to handle its population. Many residents are unable to find work or housing, and they discover that their lives are little better than they were in their home regions.

Education is one of the best examples of how life in Addis Ababa seems to offer greater opportunity, but in fact often disappoints those who come to the city seeking to improve their lives. There are far more schools in Addis Ababa than anywhere else in Ethiopia, but there are not nearly enough for all of the children who live there. Schooling is often done

*A hardware merchant sells his wares in Addis Ababa, the capital city of Ethiopia. Ethiopians often seek a better standard of living in the city.*

in three shifts a day, and classes may have as many as 120 students. Those who persist in school may have a chance to earn a scholarship to Addis Ababa University, but most students do not make it even to high school.

Though in parts of Addis Ababa there is clear evidence that a small, wealthy elite exists, it is safe to say that regardless of where the average Ethiopian lives, they do not live well by western standards. Life is very hard and, for most, relatively short. Infant mortality is high, and those who survive to adulthood usually live only into their early fifties. The strains of the everyday struggle simply to stay alive take a toll. Still, like the beautiful embroidered borders of their traditional *shammas,* there are splashes of color, and hints of a cultural richness and depth even among the poorest of Ethiopians, which can be seen wherever one looks, from the Danakil Depression to Revolution Square.

# THE CHALLENGES OF A NEW CENTURY

In one way or another, most of the problems facing Ethiopia today are tied to one simple fact: Many of its people are starving. Since the early 1980s, Ethiopia has been hit by a series of droughts centered in its low-lying regions, and in a country that struggles to support itself even in good years, a long period of drought is particularly devastating. When people are hungry, all aspects of society are affected. This struggle for survival rekindles historic animosities among people who had learned over time to get along with each other and causes a loss of faith in the government's ability to lead the nation out of crisis.

With hunger also comes a hopelessness about the future, which gets in the way of individuals and families finding solutions to their problems. Such long-range goals as getting an education, participating in politics and government, and making improvements on homes and farms are largely irrelevant to people who are living on the brink of starvation. Many live in refugee camps set up by the government for people who have abandoned their parched farmland or are "cloud chasing," a term used for walking every day to the point of exhaustion toward dark clouds that hold a usually false hope of rain. As with any major disaster facing a group or an individual, the end of the immediate crisis actually will resolve very little. Ethiopians, the majority of whom are young enough to have known nothing but drought, are psychologically scarred and physically uprooted. The 2000 rainy season brought rainfall, but it will take more than rainfall to put Ethiopia back on its feet.

## THE CAUSES OF FAMINE
The main challenge of life in contemporary Ethiopia is finding a means to hold the country together until the drought ends.

But when this will happen is difficult to predict. According to researchers for the Library of Congress, the current crisis began in 1969, when, "Dry weather swept eastward through the Horn of Africa [and] by 1973 the attendant famine had threatened the lives of hundreds of thousands of Ethiopian nomads, who had to leave their home grounds and struggle into Somalia, Djibouti, Kenya, and Sudan, seeking relief from starvation."[29] In 1973 alone, approximately 300,000 peasants died in Ethiopia, and large numbers of survivors crowded into Addis Ababa and other towns equally ill equipped to handle the influx. According to the Library of Congress study, "Ethiopia had never recovered from [this] famine . . . when the late 1970s again brought signs of intensifying drought."[30] A third period of drought began in the mid-1980s, aggravated by severe grasshopper and locust infestations that destroyed what little plant life had managed to grow.

*Refugees wrap the corpse of a famine victim at a camp in Korem.*

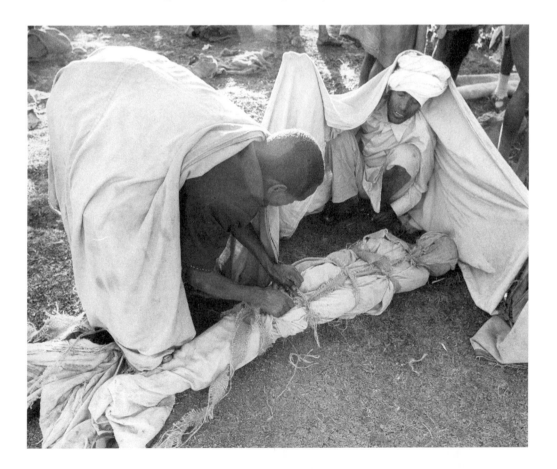

However, the drought in and of itself would not necessarily have caused the devastation that ensued. Prompt action to begin relief efforts and a farsighted approach to preparations for future years of drought were needed, but the Mengistu government appeared completely indifferent to the plight of its citizens. By 1986, according to the authors of *Ethiopia: A Country Study,* "the combined effects of famine and internal war had . . . put the nation's economy into a state of collapse,"[31] a state it has remained in ever since.

The Mengistu government's use of the drought and the famine that ensued as a tool to suppress opposition and to break centuries old farming traditions made the situation much worse. "Many peasants fled rather than submit to relocation [and] the government in most cases failed to provide the promised services"[32] such as water, schools, medical services, and food supply points to those who relocated in planned villages. Living in villages wasted time and precious energy because weakened and hungry peasants often spent hours each day just walking to and from the fields they were attempting to cultivate. Thus overall, the programs of the Mengistu government, implemented at a time of national crisis, set in motion inefficient or unworkable new realities. This in turn began a period of unrest, lack of confidence, and in some regions hostility toward the centralized government of Ethiopia, a situation that continues today. Lack of confidence that the government—or anyone else for that matter—can solve Ethiopia's problems is perhaps the most important indicator of how far the country needs to go to get back on its feet.

## THE STRAINS OF URBANIZATION

Library of Congress researchers report that Ethiopia is "under-urbanized, even by African standards."[33] This means that surprisingly few people live in cities, and that activities associated with cities, such as industry and trade, are also lacking. Modern nations need a broad base for their economy, which involves having both prosperous cities and farms. This "under-urbanization," especially when combined with a weak agricultural base is what has made Ethiopia one of the poorest nations on earth.

Warfare in the provinces in recent years has created a steady stream of people seeking the relative calm of Addis Ababa and smaller cities. There, lack of adequate housing, access to water,

*Residents of Addis Ababa often suffer from inadequate housing and poor access to water.*

and social services such as clinics and schools have created an unpleasant, unhealthy environment for the vast majority of Ethiopians who have left their villages to seek a better life in the country's population centers. Only a very small number of Ethiopians live what would be called a comfortable life by western standards. The vast majority are desperately poor, regardless of where they live.

## ETHNIC RELATIONSHIPS

In Ethiopia, poverty crosses all ethnic lines. According to the Library of Congress, this is partly because "Ethnicity in Ethiopia is an enormously complex concept."[34] The Amhara, found primarily on the western plateau, are historically and culturally the most dominant group. Over the centuries the Solomonic rulers, themselves Amharic, absorbed and intermingled with other groups so that being Amharic became less and less a purely ethnic designation and more a sign of social prestige. Other than the lowland nomadic peoples, who keep as much to themselves as possible, the only group that did not seek prestige by association with the Amhara was the Tigrayans. Proud of the fact that the founding Ethiopian empire, Aksum, was centered in Tigray, and wary of the historic dominance of the Amhara, many Tigrayans today continue to assert their ethnic separateness.

Some observers today feel that ethnic separateness represents a serious threat to Ethiopia. For a united, prosperous Ethiopia to emerge, they argue, ethnicity—and the historical grudges that often go with it—must be put aside. There is no doubt that the history of the twentieth century is full of examples of Amhara efforts to unite Ethiopia culturally by forcing an Amharic identity onto the nation. The most obvious example of this is the adoption of Amharic as the national language under Haile Selassie, a move that was halted by Mengistu in favor of allowing many official languages. However, it is not practical for a nation to have no shared language with which to conduct business and run the government, and Amharic has remained, practically speaking, the official language of the country. The unfortunate legacy of Haile Selassie and Mengistu is deeply felt mistrust across ethnic lines.

Ethnic conflicts continue to characterize Ethiopia today. The Oromo and Somali are becoming more assertive about establishing greater autonomy. For example, many Somali feel strongly that a Greater Somalia is more culturally and geographically valid than a Greater Ethiopia in the Horn of Africa region. But, as historian Harold G. Marcus writes, "If Ethiopia is to survive . . . its peoples must feel that their cultures and

## WOMEN'S RIGHTS

Women in Ethiopia endure shocking violations of what most of the rest of the world see as basic human rights. According to nurse Aregash Ayele, interviewed by Panafrican News Agency reporter Youhannes Rupphael for the news service Africa News Online, women "have to have permission from their husbands to come to us" for medical care at rural clinics. But this is mild in comparison to some of the ritual abuses inflicted upon Ethiopian women, particularly in rural areas. For example, among the Hamar people, when a young man celebrates puberty, part of the ceremony involves a selected female family member enduring a whipping that leaves her badly scarred. These whippings are repeated as each male child reaches puberty, and a completely scarred back is seen as a sign of family honor.

The most notable problem affecting the mental and physical health of most Ethiopian women, however, is the continued practice of female genital mutilation, sometimes called female circumcision. In this operation, usually performed on young girls before puberty, the clitoris is cut away so that as adults they will have little or no ability to enjoy sex. This procedure is believed to protect their chastity while unmarried and make them faithful wives later.

Some sources claim that 90 percent of Ethiopian girls undergo this procedure, which is generally done in unsanitary conditions without anesthetic. Long-term pain or infection and even death sometimes result from the procedure.

languages are being safeguarded by the government. Cultural and political autonomy must be respected as a matter of right. Otherwise the state will split apart as the minorities compete for power."[35] Ethiopia watchers say the region will best be able to prosper if the different groups find a way to work together, rather than splintering into a number of small, competing, and often hostile nations. Ethiopia, despite its problems, is still the dominant power in the region, and it would be potentially disastrous if the nation disintegrated under pressures from its ethnic groups or if the nations forming the Horn of Africa cannot, in the words of Marcus, "relearn the lost art of compromise. . . . Historically, Ethiopia and its neighbors have lived together fruitfully when ideological or ethnic concerns have been muted. When, however, religion, politics, or economic factors have become dominating and unbalancing, the entire region has fallen into mayhem."[36]

A case in point is the recent renewal of hostilities between now-independent Eritrea and Ethiopia over how to deliver aid shipments to drought-stricken Ethiopians. The Ethiopian government does not want to use Eritrean ports in part because it is involved in a violent border dispute with that country and in part because it claims that ill will between the two nations results in shipments being confiscated or otherwise badly handled. Though this issue has been resolved by resorting to other ports such as Djibouti, such lack of cooperation and trust in the end hurts the innocent people of the region and contributes to continued instability.

## HEALTH CARE

One of the major sources of overall national weakness and instability in Ethiopia is the poor health of its citizens. Due to the isolation of many of its citizens in rural regions, what health care services the nation can afford are difficult to deliver. In fact, the mere absence of roads has been a factor in the number of people who have died of starvation and disease in recent years simply because supplies could not reach them in time. Likewise, efforts to immunize people against diseases such as meningitis have been hampered by the difficulty of getting vaccines requiring refrigeration to villages as much as a three-day journey from the nearest clinic. Added to that, low literacy rates among the remote rural populations make it difficult to get information about health issues to those who need it most.

Though the Mengistu regime is considered overall to be a dark period in Ethiopian history, Mengistu at least planned and even started programs to solve some of the health and other issues affecting rural Ethiopians. A plan to provide trained health workers in remote regions failed primarily because of problems training adequate numbers of personnel to cover the sparsely populated rural regions in a way that would make medical service no more than a day away. Programs to vaccinate and to provide preventative care were more effective in cities and towns, but that is not where the vast majority of Ethiopians live.

Health care in rural areas is still seriously lacking today, and services in urban areas are grossly inadequate, although progress is made each year. It is estimated that three-quarters of rural Ethiopians, and more than 60 percent of Ethiopians overall, still do not have easily accessible clinics. The latest official statistics indicate that there are fewer than six hundred physicians in the country, a ratio of roughly one physician for every seventy-five thousand people—one of the worst in the world.

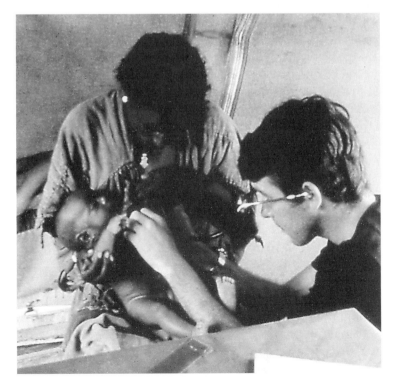

*A doctor cares for his patient. Approximately 60 percent of Ethiopia's population lacks adequate health care.*

*British relief workers measure children's arms to determine their degree of starvation, and which ones will receive immediate aid.*

As a result, Ethiopia's main health problems are, according to the Library of Congress, "communicable diseases caused by poor sanitation and malnutrition and exacerbated by the shortage of trained manpower and health facilities."[37] Reports from groups such as the World Health Organization (WHO) and the United Nations International Children's Emergency Fund (UNICEF) indicate that 60 percent of childhood deaths are preventable. Children routinely die of diarrhea, complications from colds, skin and eye infections, and fevers. Adults also succumb to preventable or treatable illnesses such as dysentery, parasitic worms, malaria, sexually transmitted diseases, tuberculosis, tetanus, and hepatitis. When water suitable for drinking is available only to approximately 14 percent of the population, it is no surprise that intestinal parasites and other waterborne health problems take thousands of lives each year. AIDS also is growing in Ethiopia, from two known cases in 1986 to around 3 million today, or 10 percent of the sexually active population.

## EDUCATION

The Mengistu regime was somewhat more successful in implementing literacy and primary education programs than it was in improving health care. Though statistical reports vary widely, it seems fairly accurate to say that literacy has gone up from 10 percent under Haile Selassie to 35 percent today.

A national literacy campaign began in 1975 when approximately sixty thousand literate students were sent to rural regions to teach residents—adults and children alike—to read in Amharic, Oromo, Tigrinya, Welamo, or Somali. The government also supplied reading materials on practical topics such as agriculture and health—and materials praising the Mengistu regime—for those who had learned to read.

Though the sixty thousand people were considered to have volunteered, Mengistu had recently closed Haile Selassie University in Addis Ababa as well as all government funded high schools in the country, leaving many young people and teachers with little else to do. What on the surface seems a rather odd move made sense on other levels. Mengistu felt that a leveling of opportunity was important and that the privileged should give of their time, in the short run at least, to help their fellow citizens. Mengistu's primary motive was undoubtedly political. He hoped to curb dissent, which generally begins among groups of bright, educated young people, by breaking up the school communities in which their dissent might take voice and grow. Whatever the motive, many Ethiopians were able to read as a result of this literacy campaign and thus might at least potentially become more involved and productive citizens.

*An overcrowded high school classroom in Ethiopia.*

## ELECTIONS, ETHIOPIAN STYLE

In May 2000 Ethiopia prepared for its first elections since the establishment of the government of President Negasso Gidada and Prime Minister Meles Zenawi in August 1995. Free and open elections are a new phenomenon in Ethiopia, and both government- and opposition-party campaign tactics have created controversy in a culture which is not yet confident that the democratic process can work for them.

Reporter Mesay Temtimie interviewed a number of candidates and election observers for his May 2000 article "The Battle for Tolerance" for Africa News Online and found much cynicism mixed with the hope that the elections would go smoothly and result in a government with the strong support of the people. One candidate, Haile Dellello, recently quit his race for a seat in the legislatures, commenting, "Although I respect the EPRDF [the party currently in power] for it has brought electric light, water and telecommunications to the Damboya people, I do not even want to vote for it. I just want to be free."

Other political candidates have focused on undermining their opponents, creating a divisiveness that alarms many observers. Some groups have been more militant, resorting to coercion and fear to derail the process and increase political instability. One candidate comments,

The government's goals in regard to educating the young were to increase the number of primary schools and, to a lesser extent, junior high and high schools. Over four hundred new schools were opened annually during the Mengistu regime, and the number of students served tripled. However, typical of Mengistu, in areas of revolt and insurgency, such as Eritrea and Tigray, the number of primary schools actually declined. The number of junior high and high schools doubled as well during the Mengistu era. However, as was the case with many Mengistu programs, a good idea was poorly planned and implemented. Although there were far more schools and pupils, there was not a corresponding number of new teachers, and by the mid-1980s, secondary teachers routinely had so many students that they could hardly be effective at teaching them. Also, though 3.1 million students were enrolled at all grade levels by 1986, up from 785,000 nationwide a decade before, the statistics belied the fact that still

It is said that my party burns houses, destroys infrastructure, etc., but all these are mere fabrications by the EPRDF . . . for the purpose of winning the election. Other candidates feel that the government has sabotaged their campaigns. EPRDF candidates are infringing on our rights, [blocking us] from running for no apparent reason.

An EPRDF candidate counters by saying, "We would like to call to the attention of opposition parties that we [should] take our alternatives and our programs to the society peacefully and hear the verdict from there." He is confident that the positive changes in the lives of farmers will result in victory for his party.

Often obscured amid the clamor are the voices of independent candidates such as Aboche Takiso.

I belong to a peasant family and I feel the pulse [of my people]. People face so many problems. I do not want to promise what I cannot fulfill. I know that the Hosanna - Addis gravel road is very inconvenient; however it would be ridiculous for me to say I would have it upgraded. My motto is standing politically for one Ethiopia. I oppose the setting up of organizations along ethnic lines, because this is divisive."

less than half of Ethiopia's grade school age children and only 5 percent of high school age students were in school. Today the situation has not changed dramatically because of other more pressing priorities brought on by famine and ethnic hostilities within Ethiopia and with its neighbors.

Opportunities for higher education at the college and university level and to participate in vocational training programs have increased in recent years, but they remain rare. Haile Selassie University reopened recently as Addis Ababa University and is one of two major universities in the country. Graduate degrees in medicine, agriculture, and engineering can now be earned in Ethiopia, although it is still more common for Ethiopian students to travel abroad to study at this level. Ethiopia has a polytechnic institute where students learn agricultural mechanics, industrial chemistry, and other technologies. Secondary students who do not plan to attend college may opt for specialized training in needed technological and industrial fields while in high school, so they may go directly to work as a skilled laborer. The government also funds twelve special peasant training centers in rural areas where people may take three-week to six-month courses in subjects relating to agriculture and land management.

## LAND REFORM

The emphasis on agricultural training and development is sorely needed in a country where decades of ill-conceived land reform and development programs worsened problems caused by repeated crop failures. Until the 1974 revolution that overthrew Haile Selassie, land ownership and use had not changed much since medieval times. Though there were a documented 111 types of land ownership and tenancy, a few systems are of particular note. The first, *rist*, was a system by which ownership of land remained in a family rather than any individual. Land could not be sold, given, or mortgaged because it belonged in a family forever. The second, *gult*, was a system whereby the emperor gave land to nobles or other loyal supporters as a reward or to government officials in place of salary. People who lived and farmed on the land did not own it but rather became tenants who owed rent and taxes to the *gult* owner.

These two systems were very different. *Rist* created a sense of ownership and security among the peasants, whereas *gult* bred resentment, apathy toward developing land and producing good yields, and insecurity about the future. Thus, when the Mengistu government announced its plans to reclaim ownership of all land by the government but return to each peasant family what were called "possessing rights" to a small plot of land adequate to meet its needs, the reaction varied widely. Those who struggled under the *gult* system were very positive about throwing off oppressive landlords, but those who held land under the *rist* system saw that the new concept of "possessing rights" was far less desirable than a hereditary, permanent right to their land.

Mengistu insisted that he had no interest in upsetting the centuries-old traditions of small subsistence farms. He claimed he was giving all Ethiopian peasants a chance to "own" one, but it quickly became apparent that the regime wanted peasants to join cooperatives, where farmers pool their land and equipment, work together, and share both the risks and the profits. According to the Library of Congress, "The government provided a number of inducements to producers' cooperatives, including priority for credits, fertilizers, improved seed, and access to consumer items and building materials."[38] Mengistu felt that larger farms would improve yields and make the country more able to feed itself and even increase export crops such as coffee for much needed profits.

He turned out to be wrong. Though large farming cooperatives received most of the government subsidies, including three-quarters of the fertilizers, and almost all of the best hybrid seeds, subsistence farmers still produced 90 percent of the crops. In a country with such difficult conditions for farming, so far the old ways still seem to work best. However, the current government is committed to the idea of retaining state ownership and control of all land, a policy that has created much unrest and mistrust among Ethiopians today. Its leaders will need to realize that a slow and very thoughtful approach, one supported by the Ethiopian people, is likely to work better than sweeping visions and quick fixes.

*Two men work together to harvest teff, a grain unique to Ethiopia*

## RESETTLEMENT AND VILLAGIZATION

Another sweeping vision and quick fix that yielded disastrous results was the resettlement program. Under Mengistu millions of people were forcibly relocated from drought stricken areas to other parts of Ethiopia where arable, or farmable, land was more plentiful. He ignored people's traditional attachment to their lands, did not take into account how people who lived in the proposed resettlement areas would take to the sudden influx of outsiders, and did not properly prepare the support services needed to feed, house, and clothe the refugees. Most Ethiopians, and the world community as a whole, saw resettlement as a political ploy to break up strongholds of resistance, but because only

15 percent of the relocated were from Tigray and none were from Eritrea, it does not appear that this was Mengistu's initial or primary motive.

Villagization, the attempt under Mengistu to pull a number of tiny villages of half a dozen families into larger ones of two to three hundred was similarly disruptive of traditional

## BUILDING A STRONGER ETHIOPIA

In recent years many projects have been undertaken in Ethiopia, both by the government and by private consortia and individuals, to develop a more diverse economy, promote better health, and improve agriculture. Bringing more money into the country through profitable exports, decreasing the risk of calamities caused by crop failures, and improving the productivity of its people are all considered essential to building a profitable and competitive economy and thus a brighter future for Ethiopia. Some of the more notable projects by Ethiopians for Ethiopians under way in the year 2000 included the following:

Twelve entrepreneurs made a multimillion dollar investment in Tigray for mineral resources development. Early on their project created over four hundred new jobs. The focus of this project is the development of mining of marble, granite, and other attractive stones used to decorate buildings.

In eastern Shewa, approximately thirty private organizations were working on projects designed to improve both the amount of and the delivery systems for drinkable water in rural areas. They were also building irrigation systems and small dams for water collection and conservation. Elsewhere in Ethiopia similar government and privately funded projects to increase access to water succeeded in increasing the amount of land available for irrigation as well as water suitable for sanitation and drinking.

A government-funded agricultural extension program designed to increase and improve farmable land has reached 2.7 million farmers, providing many tons of fertilizer, seeds, coffee seedlings, and other needed supplies. Additionally, four thousand rural stations had been established to provide information and technical assistance to farmers.

In one region, nearly a thousand miles of new roads were built and another thousand miles were renovated. It is anticipated that the existence of these roads will indirectly create as many as fifty thousand new jobs as a result of increased commerce.

life. Poor planning resulted in increases in communicable diseases, lowered yields on farms, and increased dependence on government assistance for survival. In early 1990 Mengistu announced his abandonment of the idea, but the damage was already done for the 13 million Ethiopians who had been villagized. These and other similar attempts to transform and tightly control life in Ethiopia, though now abandoned, have cast a long shadow. A thoroughly disrupted culture now finds itself struggling to survive blistering drought without the comfort and security of home and traditional ways. One of the challenges of the current era will be not so much to restore the old ways intact but retain what is necessary and valuable and take advantage of the breaks with tradition to introduce improvements in a sensitive and well-planned way.

## PROTECTING THE ENVIRONMENT

In some respects it may be easier to undo damage done to people than the damage of the last century to the land itself. Two related problems known as desertification and deforestation will make it more difficult for Ethiopia to improve its agricultural base. Deforestation refers to the cutting of large stretches of timber either to make room for agriculture or for use in building. It often leads to desertification, a term used for land that has become desertlike as a result of poor land use such as overplanting or clear-cutting. At the turn of the twentieth century, 30 percent of Ethiopia was forests. Now forests cover less than 4 percent of the country. According to the Library of Congress, "The northern parts of the highlands are almost devoid of trees."[39] Ethiopia will soon need to turn its attention to its renewable resources, but as is often the case with countries in crisis, it is difficult to think about things like trees when people are suffering.

In fact, it is difficult to think about anything else when people are suffering. The greatest challenge facing Ethiopia's leaders today will be to retain a sense of vision and future orientation while dealing with innumerable serious problems both within and outside the country's borders. Recent developments such as a massive road building campaign in Tigray are taken by many as hopeful signs that the country will develop what it needs to support itself and once again reclaim its ancient place as one of the world's great countries.

# 6
# "WAX AND GOLD": THE ARTS AND ENTERTAINMENT IN ETHIOPIA

For centuries Ethiopian goldsmiths have practiced the ancient art of lost wax casting, in which clay is molded around a wax model of the desired shape, and molten gold is then poured into a hole on the top of the mold. The wax melts and is replaced by the gold in the same shape as the wax. When the gold has cooled, the mold is smashed and the finished piece is trimmed and polished. Ethiopians see symbolism in this process, whereby something of little obvious value (the wax model) is replaced by something of great value (the gold casting), and they use the metaphor of "wax and gold" to refer to art where a shallow and a deeper meaning exist side by side.

In cultures that have suffered from government censorship and suppression of the arts, as was the case in twentieth-century Ethiopia under Haile Selassie and Mengistu, it is common to express criticism and protest through the arts. But these expressions are often veiled, with the superficial meaning dribbling out like lost wax and the real meaning left behind in solid form. The concept of art being like "wax and gold" did not develop in this recent period of political oppression, however, but centuries ago in connection to a particular kind of poetry. The continued use of the ancient term "wax and gold" serves as a good example, therefore, of Ethiopians' reverence for the traditional and their continued strong emphasis on the past in the art of the present day. In fact it is difficult to call any Ethiopian art thoroughly "modern" or "contemporary" because all of the arts build so extensively on the models of the past.

The name "wax and gold," or *sam-enna-warq* was given centuries ago to a particular kind of poem in which a hidden meaning exists behind a superficial one. Ethiopians today still write *sam-enna-warq* poems and songs, and their slogans and expressions tend to have several levels of meaning as well. For example, an Ethiopian might say it is good to send one's enemies off with coffee. On the surface this might sound like good hospitality, but it also means not to bother wasting anything more expensive or precious on them. Also when the Amharic words for "send off with coffee" are said quickly they sound very much like "turn to ashes," implying that the thing to do to an enemy is destroy him. The Amhara in particular love these sly word tricks and are particularly proud of their long literary traditions of which *sam-enna-warq* is only a part. Likewise, song lyrics may on the surface sound as if they are about an abused lover but are in fact about resenting political oppression, as these words from a song of the Haile Selassie era demonstrate:

I can't take it any more. I've had enough.

I can't put up with your torments

I don't know what more I can do.[40]

## LITERATURE

Interestingly, the first literature in Ethiopia was not intended to criticize those in power but to glorify them. Written work in Ge'ez dates from after the short interlude of the Zagwe dynasty, at the time of the restoration of the Solomonic dynasty. The emperors were eager to establish their hereditary right to the throne of Ethiopia because of their kinship with the great king Solomon, and they sponsored works of literature that told purportedly factual stories about this lineage. The fourteenth-century *Kebre Negast,* which relates the story of Solomon and Sheba among other things, is considered the first work of Ethiopian literature. Other works followed, many of them religious, detailing the lives of saints and documenting church songs and practices.

As elsewhere in Africa, lack of opportunities to publish set back the development of a strong national literature in the twentieth century. Today, however, that is being addressed by such eminent novelists as Sahle Selassie, whose most famous work is *Shinega's Village: Scenes of Ethiopian Life*

(1964), followed in 1974 by *Warrior King* and in 1979 by *Fire-brands*. Berhanov Zerihun is another well-known modern author. The best-known modern playwright is Tsegaye Gabre-Madhin, whose play *Oda-Oak Oracle: A Legend of Black Peoples, Told of God and God, of Hope and Love, and of Fear and Sacrifices,* published in English in 1965, has as its theme the tensions between superstition and reason in the lives of rural Ethiopians.

## VISUAL ARTS

Visual arts such as painting also have very early origins in Ethiopia, and like literature, they tend to remain tied to traditional styles. Ethiopian painting has its origins in the church. Artists painted directly on the rock walls and ceilings of churches and caves used for meditation and worship, and they also used wood or parchment for movable works of art. The style from the very beginning was meant to be symbolic

## THE SORGHUM SCULPTURES OF TOLERA TAFA

In the small roadside village of Necho approximately forty miles west of Addis Ababa, an art form has evolved that shows that Ethiopians value not only the artistic traditions of the past but also new ideas. Tolera Tafa and others in his village have developed a form of sculpture using discarded stalks of the sorghum plant, a cereal crop grown in the area. They use razor blades and their teeth to strip, shape, and construct elaborate models of churches, ships, trucks, and other objects, using no glue or any other product but the sorghum stalks themselves.

The sturdiness of the overall constructions impress those who see them, but the real wonder of the sculptures is their remarkable detail. For example, an approximately eighteen-inch-long model of an Ethiopian *wiyiyyit,* a truck converted for use as a taxi, comes complete with steering wheel, windshield wipers, radio antenna, headlights, license plates, and a jump seat, as well as doors that open and wheels that spin. Tolera's helicopters have a cockpit seat, control sticks, and spinning propeller blades, and his dump trucks have beds that go up and down. His churches have slatted windows, made from hair thin strips of sorghum, and beautiful porches and steeples.

rather than realistic. For example, important people are painted larger than others, even if they are standing right next to them. Eyes are of particular importance, and they are often drawn on their own as decorations on doors or entryways. As parts of faces, eyes of good people such as saints usually look straight forward at the viewer, while the single eye of a profile view is used to depict figures representing bad or evil. Eyes are often painted much larger than they really are in comparison to other facial features, as a way of emphasizing what eyes are believed to say about a person's character.

Traditionally, Ethiopian church painters tried to decorate every bit of wall space, leading to a style that emphasizes geometric designs and other space fillers such as crosses. Painters tended to choose the brightest pigments they could find, resulting in finished works that are striking in their use of brilliant greens, reds, blues, and yellows. In recent years, these traditional styles have been adapted to different art

Tolera Tafa modestly dismisses the artistry of what he does. In fact, Neal W. Sobania reports in *Ethiopia: Traditions of Creativity* that Tolera gives so little thought to the artistic value of his trucks and churches that "the question of whether [he] had ever given one to his mother as a gift to display was particularly strange." Though he is recognized as the best practitioner of this local art form, Tolera claims in an interview with Sobania that among sorghum sculptors, "We only compete for dollars." It takes a little less than a day to make most models, and they fetch prices ranging from approximately two dollars if sold by the road to five dollars in Addis Ababa. Larger, more elaborate models may fetch up to thirty dollars. These modest profits have been sufficient for Tolera to build his parents a new house and finance his return to school to complete the tenth grade as he nears age thirty.

His hope is to study engineering or architecture, but opportunities are rare to fulfill such dreams. He may end up as his friends have, continuing to churn out models to sell by the road, but recent commissions to do models of the White House and Jefferson Memorial, the Leaning Tower of Pisa, and other famous buildings may mean that an international reputation, and thus higher price tags for his work, are around the corner. In that case, sorghum sculpture may become one of the many original art forms to come out of Africa in recent years and take the art world by storm.

*A nineteenth-century Ethiopian painting depicts Mary and Child with Archangels and Donors.*

forms with great success. Perhaps the best example is Afew-erk Tekle's stained glass windows entitled *Yesterday's Today's and Tomorrow's Africa* in Addis Ababa's Africa Hall. The faces in these intensely colored windows look out at the viewer with the same huge eyes as can be found in the rock churches, and although the windows incorporate modern-looking backgrounds and contemporary history, the overall effect is still clearly respectful of ancient traditions.

Other internationally known painters in modern Ethiopia include Zerihun Yetmgeta, Gebre Kristos Desta, Skunder Boghossian, Goshu Wolde, and Desta Hagos. Most paint in styles strongly influenced by western art but tend to use Ethiopian themes, history, and traditions as their subject matter. One of the most original, and perhaps the best known of these artists worldwide, is Zerihun Yetmgeta. Although he works in many media, including wood engraving and collages, he is best known for his bamboo strip paintings meant to evoke the ancient tradition of magic scrolls. Magic scrolls were strips of parchment on which were painted prayers and images such as angels, crosses, and eyes. In his modern version, Zerihun combines images of ancient Ethiopia with modern images of rockets and computer chips, to tell stories about Ethiopia's past, present, and future.

Desta Hagos, who specializes in beautiful paintings of nature, is also particularly notable because she is one of the few female professional artists in Ethiopia. The School of Fine Arts in Addis Ababa is the main center where artists go to study and practice their art, and though women, including Desta Hagos, have studied there, their numbers are still small. This is the result of the difficulties women have gaining the kind of support they need from family and patrons to choose a life as an artist.

## DECORATIVE ARTS

Women are better represented in the decorative arts such as basket weaving and pottery because many of these art forms are traditionally seen as women's work. Other decorative arts, such as metalwork, wood carving, and leather working, are considered men's work. Together, Ethiopian men and women have created one of the most diverse and remarkable traditions of decorative art in all of Africa. Ethiopian basketry and jewelry are particularly valued on the world market today, especially those pieces that convey a strong sense of continuity of tradition. For example, one Borana basket weaver, Elema Boru, is acclaimed for her ability to produce outstanding examples of the traditional Borana milk container—a closed container woven so tightly it does not leak.

Two highly reputed silversmiths, Gezahegn Gebre Yohannes and Abib Sa'id are among the hundreds who continue to produce religious items such as crosses as well as personal jewelry by traditional means such as hammering, welding, engraving, and the lost wax method. Though silver is today the most common metal, gold, copper, and other alloys are also commonly used in Ethiopian jewelry and religious artifacts.

Many of the pieces made today are for tourists or for export to foreign markets, but Ethiopians themselves highly value the jewelry made by their countrymen. They tend to place less value on other art forms such as basketry and wood carving, because these items are more functional in daily life, and thus their beauty often goes unnoticed. In Ethiopia, writes art historian Raymond A. Silverman, there is a saying that "gold in one's hand is like copper."[41] In other words, it is often difficult to value properly the things one has

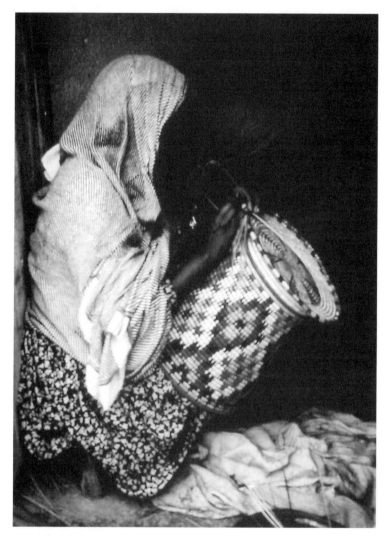

or sees on a daily basis. Still, as more and more foreigners express their appreciation and are willing to show it by paying high prices for simple objects, the people of Ethiopia are beginning to respond, giving hope that the artistic products of rural Ethiopia can provide at least a partial solution to the serious economic problems of the country.

## MUSICAL TRADITION IN ETHIOPIA

As in literature, the visual arts, and the decorative arts, music in Ethiopia today draws heavily on tradition. In fact, according to musicologist Peter Manuel, "The nation's own musical heritage . . . constitutes one of the world's most ancient continuous musical traditions."[42] Although it has borrowed from Arabic and other African musical styles over the centuries and is influenced by western music available on cassettes or heard on the radio, today a distinct Ethiopian sense of melody, instrumentation, and rhythm continues.

This uniqueness is due to Ethiopia's relative isolation from other countries for many centuries. Ethiopians, for example, had diverged in beliefs and practices from Roman Catholic and Orthodox Christians by the middle of the first millennium, and the music used in worship had diverged as well. Ethiopian Christian church services traditionally are almost entirely sung, and thus by approximately A.D. 500, unique musical styles had begun to evolve in this religious setting. Instruments such as a drum called a *kebero* and rattles called *sistrums* or *tsenatsels* have played prominent roles in church services for many centuries, helping to control the rhythm and pace of music in the way an organ might do in a western church.

*Ethiopian priests play musical instruments such as the* kebero *(drum) and* sistrums *(rattles) during worship services.*

Nonchurch music has also taken unique forms in Ethiopia for centuries. Instruments such as the *washint,* a four-holed wooden flute; the *begenna,* a kind of harp; the *masenqo,* a one-stringed fiddle played with a bow like a violin; and a banjolike instrument called a *krar* are central to Ethiopian music and are found nowhere else. In rural Ethiopia it is common for villagers to make simple instruments such as these and become skilled at playing them as a way to pass time while watching the herds or waiting for harvest.

Music is a part of everyday life for Ethiopians, but as elsewhere in Africa, traditions rarely involve concert-style music. In Ethiopia, the audience participates by clapping and dancing and by singing along in what is generally referred to as call-and-response. In call-and-response the performers sing or say something to the audience and the audience is expected to sing or say something back. Likewise, most Ethiopians see a piece of music as incomplete if they are not doing the dance they associate with it. A good example of the Ethiopian approach to music is *zanfan,* an improvised song and dance involving clapping and shoulder shaking and simple cries such as "lay-lay-lay" while singers are making up elaborate and often satirical verses about events that have just occurred. Rural Ethiopians may make up such songs for any occasion, from one as ordinary as going to market to something more special, such as a victory in an athletic contest.

Though Ethiopians generally see music as a shared activity created by everyone—performer and audience alike—there are nevertheless some special classes of musicians who perform solo. For example, the *debteras,* or church musicians, are responsible for specific chants and other musical accompaniment that only they perform. Two other kinds of musicians, the *azmaris* and the *lalibalotch,* also perform alone. The *azmaris* wander about the countryside singing both sentimental songs about love and biting commentaries on political events. The *lalibalotch* often are afflicted with leprosy, which destroys flesh and hideously disfigures its victims. Because the disease is contagious, lepers may not normally mix with the public but are permitted outside in the early morning to sing and beg for coins or food.

## Ethiopian Music Today

As in many other countries, the popular music of today's Ethiopia is derived from traditional dances and songs of musicians such as the *azmaris*. According to Peter Manuel, "Particularly important as a source [is] the music sung at weddings and other festivities to the accompaniment of the *kvar* (lyre) and *kebero* (drum)."[43] Traditional elements that distinguish Ethiopian music are a singing style that sounds rather tight, high, and nasal by western standards, and melodies that feature very elaborate vocals. A singer might, for instance, stretch a word or a phrase out over many notes, rising to a very high pitch before descending to a very low one. The scales used are different from the western one, usually consisting of only five notes spaced farther apart than those on the western scales. These scales, called "pentatonic," or five-tone, are associated with church music. According to musicologist Francis Falceto, the "limping, asymmetrical rhythms" and

*An Ethiopian woman plays her homemade drum.*

large intervals between some of the notes give "an unresolved feeling to the music, like missing your foot on the
stairs in the dark or waiting for a stone to hit the bottom
of a well and not hearing it."[44]

When Ethiopian music is called modern, what is generally meant is that traditional instruments have been sup-
plemented or replaced by western instruments such as

## ASTER AWEKE

Aster Aweke has been for the last two decades
one of the best-known Ethiopian musical stars. She was born
in Gonder in 1961, the daughter of a high-ranking official in
Haile Selassie's government. She first began singing in 1977
with different groups and solo. Her career took off when music
entrepreneur Ali Tango heard her sing and asked her to record
for him. She joined the Roha Band in 1978 and became a star
in her country. Unlike some of her counterparts, she left
Ethiopia in the early 1980s, settling in Washington, D.C. and
making a living singing in clubs. But her talent did not stay
unnoticed in the United States for long, and her impassioned
vocal style soon earned her a large following. She continues to
record best-sellers, modifying what to many western ears are a
strained vocal style and unfamiliar sounding instrumental
arrangement to make her music more palatable to western
ears. Thus, people tend to have strong preferences either for
her earlier "purer" music or her later, high-tech, westernized
sound. But one thing that has not changed is her high-energy
singing and passionate lyrics, such as these, quoted from the
song "Yaz-oh" by *World Music: The Rough Guide*:

Ayee—get it on

Ayee—like this, like that

Don't tell anybody, keep it to yourself

How can I keep a secret?

I am in love with you

But don't tell anybody, keep it to yourself

'Cause love in the open never satisfied me.

trumpets and trombones, or electric guitars. Western influences date from Haile Selassie's time, when army bands first came through Ethiopia playing western marches. According to Francis Falceto, "Progressively, private orchestras were developed, all of them evolving from an essentially military background."[45] Today's music, whether it is the type called Ethio-jazz, or accompaniment to soloists such as Aster Aweke, Neway Debebe, and Tlahoun Gessesse, tends to use instruments such as clarinets, pianos, and brass instruments, often played in ways that sound traditionally Ethiopian. Increasingly, however, Ethiopian superstars tend to have two separate bodies of music, one that relies heavily on tradition and another that is more clearly reflective of western or other African styles.

Ethiopian music was affected in several significant ways by the Mengistu dictatorship. First, Ethiopian musicians found it difficult to emigrate, and thus, unlike some of their counterparts in other parts of Africa, they formed a close-knit community within Ethiopia and developed new ideas and styles through these interactions. Francis Falceto points out that "this was the finest hour for Ephrem Tamru, Kuku Sebsebe, Netsanet Mellesse, Amelmal Abate and some fifty other singers, male and female, who wore out the three or four genuinely professional orchestras who they shared in recording sessions."[46] A more negative development came about as a result of Mengistu's curfew, which made it impossible for night clubs to stay open. Thus, the number of people playing and enjoying live music dropped to next to nothing, and the kind of creativity and enthusiasm that sparks new trends was lost for a while. Now night clubs, called *azmaribets,* are reopening to enthusiastic crowds. Falceto suggests, "Better put on your seat belt when the *eshista* or *tchik-tchik-ka* is unleashed; these are torrid dance styles in which the shaking of shoulders and chests would melt a statue."[47]

## Sports and Leisure

The athleticism of Ethiopians' favorite dances is also indicative of their general interest and skill in physical activities. This interest extends to a broad range of sports but because the country is so poor, the games Ethiopians play generally involve little or no equipment. Particularly popular are volleyball and soccer, introduced in the last few decades. One particular sport at which Ethiopians excel is distance running. Its stars include Mamo Wolde, who won the Olympic marathon in 1968, and Miruts Yifter, who won both the 5,000-meter and 10,000-meter races in the 1980 Olympic games. More recently, in 1992, Derartu Tulu, won the women's 10,000-meter Olympic gold medal.

By far the most famous and revered Ethiopian track and field star is Abebe Bikala, who won the Olympic marathon twice, in both 1960 and 1964. Abebe, a member of Haile Selassie's imperial guard, was the first black African to win the Olympic marathon, racing barefoot through the streets of

*Abebe Bikala wins the 1964 Olympic marathon. He also won the 1960 Olympic marathon, becoming the first black African to win that event.*

## Ali Tango

"Every taxi driver in Addis knows the location of Tango Music and Video Shop," Ethiopian music critic Francis Falceto writes in an article appearing in *World Music: The Rough Guide*. It is "the laboratory of national swing" and home to one of the most celebrated figures in Ethiopian music over the last few decades, Ali "Ali Tango" Kaifa.

Ali Tango spotted the commercial and cultural value of cassette tapes and brought them to Ethiopia, opening a music shop where people could buy prerecorded cassettes or make customized copies of whatever they wished. Already a producer and talent scout, Ali Tango was responsible for producing more than fifty records, which have become treasures of Ethiopian popular music, and for discovering superstars Aster Aweke and Neway Debebe. He was the first to use digital technology in the recording studio he opened in Addis Ababa.

Ali Tango is credited with being an instrumental part in keeping the recording industry going in Ethiopia during the repressive Mengistu era and, as Falceto writes, "has always defended the freedom of expression of singers and independent orchestras." He is also credited with popularizing videotape rental among those urban Ethiopians who have access to a television and a VCR. Today, most music shops in Addis also rent videotapes as a result of his sharp eye for profitable business ventures.

Rome. Four years later, only six weeks after he had his appendix removed, he set a new world and Olympic record when he won the marathon for a second time. Tragically he was later paralyzed in an automobile accident and died several years later. His funeral was attended by thousands, including many of the younger world-class runners he had inspired.

Ethiopians also enjoy playing games and sports that are uniquely their own. *Kwosso*, played with a goatskin ball, can best be compared to "keep away" played with as many as several hundred participants at once. The games tend to last all day and have few apparent rules. It is a rough sport, including tackling, butting, and collisions—all of which are done without any equipment, or indeed any clothing at all except loincloths. *Kwosso* is particularly popular in the Danakil Depression.

Another very rough game popular among the Surma is a form of stick fighting where well-padded contestants try to whack each other into submission with long wooden paddles. Occasionally people are seriously hurt, but if someone dies the person responsible is banished forever from the village. At the end of a successful match, the winner is permitted to marry the village maiden who asks him. Another game played in Ethiopia is *feres gug,* or *guks,* similar to the jousts of medieval Europe, where combatants on horseback try to knock each other to the ground with wooden poles.

Not all Ethiopian recreation is so violent. Ethiopians also love board games such as *dama,* similar to checkers. *Gabata* is another popular game much like backgammon, in which the object is to move seeds or pebbles around through a series of small depressions and in the process capture all of one's opponent's seeds or pebbles. *Kelebosh* is a popular children's game similar to jacks but played with pebbles. The game consists of tossing a pebble in the air, quickly collecting other pebbles, and catching the first pebble before it hits the ground. Hide-and-seek, or *dabebkosh,* is another favorite children's game.

The desperate life situation of so many Ethiopians affects how they spend their time. Starving people are not likely to exhaust themselves playing soccer, for example. The average Ethiopian has no access to a television and cannot read. Thus, time in Ethiopia tends to go by at a slower pace than westerners are used to because there are not as many different activities to try to fit in. Games may extend over whole afternoons. The brewing and drinking of coffee may take most of a morning. In good rainfall seasons, the work of staying alive leaves little time for leisure, and therefore Ethiopians prize their chances to relax by stretching them out as long as possible. Though they might find some amusement in things foreigners have introduced, they find by far their greatest pleasure in doing those things that best connect them with the past history of their unique nation.

# Facts About Ethiopia

## Government

Country Name: Federal Democratic Republic of Ethiopia

Capital City: Addis Ababa (population 3 million)

Government Type: Federal Republic

Executive Branch

> President: Negasso Gidada (since August 1995)
>
> Prime Minister/Head of Government: Meles Zenawi (since August 1995)
>
> Cabinet: Council of Ministers; selected by prime minister, approved by House of People's Representatives.
>
> Elections: President elected by House of People's Representatives for a six-year term (next election in 2001). Prime minister designated by majority party of House of People's Representatives.

Legislative Branch

> Bicameral Legislature:
>
>> House of Federation (upper chamber) has 117 seats; members chosen by state assemblies to serve five-year terms.
>>
>> House of People's Representatives (lower chamber) has 548 seats; members are directly elected to five-year terms by popular vote.

Judicial Branch

> Supreme Court: President and vice president of court recommended by the prime minister and appointed by the House of People's Representatives.
>
> Other Federal Courts: Prime minister submits candidates from a list selected by Federal Judicial Administrative Council. Candidates appointed, if approved by House of People's Representatives.
>
> Other Courts: Currently a transitional mix of regional and government courts.

Political Parties/Groups

> Single Party: Ethiopian People's Revolutionary Democratic Front (EPRDF)
>
> Political pressure groups:
>
>> Oromo Liberation Front (OLF)
>>
>> All Amhara People's Organization
>>
>> Southern Ethiopia People's Democratic Coalition
>>
>> numerous small, ethnically based groups

## FLAG

Three equal horizontal bands of green, yellow, and red, with a blue and
   yellow emblem in the center. Note: Ethiopia's colors have been
   adopted widely across the continent and are known as the pan-
   African colors.

## IMPORTANT HOLIDAYS

Independence Day:

None—Ethiopia and Liberia are the only African
   countries never to have been colonized.

January 7          Ethiopian Orthodox Christmas

January 19         Timkat (celebration of Christ's baptism)

September 11       Enkutatash (Festival of John the Baptist)

September 27       Maskal (Commemoration of finding of the True Cross)

## RELIGIONS

Muslim, 45–50 percent; Ethiopian Orthodox,35–40 percent; Animist
   (traditional faiths)12 percent; Other, 3–8 percent

## LANGUAGES

Amharic, Tigrinya, Orominga, Guaraginga, Somali, English (main foreign language taught in school)

## DEMOGRAPHY

Population: 55 million (1999 figures)

Ethnic Origin: Oromo, 40 percent; Amhara/Tigrean, 32 percent;
   Sidamo, 9 percent; Shankella, 6 percent; Somali, 6 percent; Afar, 4
   percent; Gurage, 2 percent; Other, 1 percent (1999 estimates)

Age Structure: 0–14 years, 46 percent; 15–64 years, 51 percent; 65 and
   over, 3 percent

Population Growth Rate: 2.16 percent

Birth Rate: 44.34 births per 1,000 population

Average Number of Births per adult female: 6.71

Death Rate: 21.43 deaths per 1,000 population

Net Migration Rate: –1.3 per 1,000 population (Note: Repatriation of
   Ethiopian refugees who fled to Sudan, Kenya, and Somalia is continuing, as is some reverse migration of those who fled the other
   direction.)

Infant Mortality Rate: 124.57 deaths per 1,000 population

Life Expectancy: total population, 40.46 years, male, 39.22 years; female, 41.73 years

Total Fertility Rate: 6.81 children born per adult woman

Literacy (age 15 and over who can read and write): total population, 35.5
   percent; male, 45.5 percent; female, 25.3 percent (1995 estimate)

## GEOGRAPHY

Area: 1,127,127 square kilometers (704,454 square miles)

Border countries: Djibouti, Eritrea, Kenya, Somalia, Sudan

Natural resources: small reserves of gold, platinum, copper, potash, natural gas

Land use: arable land, 12 percent; permanent crops, 1 percent; permanent pastures, 40 percent; forest/woodland, 25 percent; other, 22 percent

Irrigated land: 1,900 square kilometers (1,187 square miles)

Natural hazards: earthquakes, drought

Environmental issues: deforestation, overgrazing, erosion, desertification

## ECONOMY

(1998 figures)

Currency: Birr

Gross Domestic Product:

> purchasing power parity: $32.9 billion

> real growth rate: 6 percent

> per capita income: $560 per year

> composition by sector:

>> agriculture: 55 percent

>> industry: 12 percent

>> services: 35 percent

Inflation rate: 3.9 percent annually

Labor force: agriculture/animal husbandry, 80 percent; government/services, 12 percent; industry/construction, 8 percent

Industries: food processing, beverages, textile, chemicals, metal processing, cement

Agricultural products: cereals, pulses, coffee, linseed oil seed, sugarcane, potatoes, hides, cattle, sheep, goats

Exports:

> total value: $550 million

> commodities: coffee, leather products, gold, oil seed

> partners: Germany (26 percent), Japan (11 percent), Italy (10 percent), UK (8 percent)

Imports:

> total value: $1.3 billion

> commodities: food, live animals, petroleum/petroleum products, chemicals, machinery, motor vehicles, aircraft

> partners: Italy (11 percent), US (11 percent), Germany (7 percent), Saudi Arabia (4 percent)

Number of telephones: 100,000

Number of radio stations: 5

Number of radios: 9 million
Number of television stations: 25
Number of televisions: 150,000

## MILITARY

Military branches: ground forces, air force, police
Military age: 18
Military manpower availability: 13,520,300
Military expenditures as percent of budget: 2.5 percent

# Notes

## Chapter 1: Living on the Roof of Africa

1. *Ethiopia: A Country Study.* 3rd ed. Washington, DC: Library of Congress, 1993, p. xvi.

2. Philip Briggs, *Guide to Ethiopia.* Old Saybrook, CT: Globe Pequot Press, 1998, p. 259.

3. Briggs, *Guide to Ethiopia,* p. 242.

4. Briggs, *Guide to Ethiopia,* p. 228.

5. Briggs, *Guide to Ethiopia,* p. 163.

6. Quoted in John Reader, *Africa: A Biography of the Continent.* New York: Vintage Books, 1997, p. 217.

7. Kazuyoshi Nomachi, *Bless Ethiopia.* Tokyo: Odyssey Publications, 1998, p. 98.

8. Briggs, *Guide to Ethiopia,* p. 275.

9. Briggs, *Guide to Ethiopia,* p. 311.

## Chapter 2: From Lucy to the Twentieth Century

10. Reader, *Africa: A Biography of the Continent,* p. 219.

11. Harold G. Marcus, *A History of Ethiopia.* Berkeley: University of California Press, 1994, p. 12.

12. Marcus, *A History of Ethiopia,* p. 12.

13. Marcus, *A History of Ethiopia,* p. 22.

14. Marcus, *A History of Ethiopia,* p. 29.

15. Marcus, *A History of Ethiopia,* p. 34.

16. Marcus, *A History of Ethiopia,* p. 39.

17. Marcus, *A History of Ethiopia,* p. 62.

18. Marcus, *A History of Ethiopia,* p. 69.

## Chapter 3: Struggling into the Modern Era

19. Briggs, *Guide to Ethiopia,* p. 43.

20. Briggs, *Guide to Ethiopia,* p. 47.

21. Marcus, *A History of Ethiopia,* p. 190.

22. Briggs, *Guide to Ethiopia,* p. 48.

23. Marcus, *A History of Ethiopia,* p. 196.

## CHAPTER 4: DAILY LIFE IN ETHIOPIA

24. "Destination Ethiopia," Lonely Planet. www. lonelyplanet.com, p. 5.

25. "Destination Ethiopia," Lonely Planet, p. 5.

26. Nomachi, *Bless Ethiopia,* p. 63.

27. *Post Report: Ethiopia.* Washington, DC: United States Department of State, 1996, p. 1.

28. *Post Report: Ethiopia,* p. 4.

## CHAPTER 5: THE CHALLENGES OF A NEW CENTURY

29. *Ethiopia: A Country Study,* p. 87.

30. *Ethiopia: A Country Study,* p. 63.

31. *Ethiopia: A Country Study,* p. 64.

32. *Ethiopia: A Country Study,* p. 64.

33. *Ethiopia: A Country Study,* p. 82.

34. *Ethiopia: A Country Study,* p. 100.

35. Marcus, *A History of Ethiopia,* p. 219.

36. Marcus, *A History of Ethiopia,* p. 220.

37. *Ethiopia: A Country Study,* p. 136.

38. *Ethiopia: A Country Study,* p. 173.

39. *Ethiopia: A Country Study,* p. 183.

## CHAPTER 6: "WAX AND GOLD": THE ARTS AND ENTERTAINMENT IN ETHIOPIA

40. Quoted in Simon Broughton, et al. eds. *World Music: The Rough Guide.* London: Rough Guides, 1994, p. 200.

41. Raymond A. Silverman, *Ethiopia: Traditions of Creativity.* Seattle: University of Washington Press, 1999, p. 3.

42. Peter Manuel, *Popular Musics of the Non-Western World.* New York: Oxford University Press, 1988, p. 103.

43. Manuel, *Popular Musics of the Non-Western World,* p. 103.

44. Quoted in Broughton, *World Music: The Rough Guide,* p.199.

45. Quoted in Broughton, *World Music: The Rough Guide,* p. 199.

46. Quoted in Broughton, *World Music: The Rough Guide,* p. 200.

47. Quoted in Broughton, *World Music: The Rough Guide,* p. 203.

# CHRONOLOGY

**3.4 million B.C.**
*Australopithecus afarensis* ("Lucy") inhabits region of today's Danakil Depression.

**8000 B.C.**
Inhabitants of Ethiopia have domesticated sheep and cattle.

**3000 B.C.**
Inhabitants of Ethiopia have begun cultivating teff and *ensete*.

**2000 B.C.**
Inhabitants of Ethiopia are using plows to cultivate land.

**500 B.C.**
Establishment of Aksumite empire.

**4th century A.D.**
According to tradition, Frumentius and Aedisius bring Christianity to Aksum.

**6th century**
Falasha (black Jews) settle in Gonder.

**7th century**
Islam comes to Horn of Africa.

**ca. 750**
Drought undermines Aksumite empire.

**9th century**
Judith (Yodit) sacks Aksum; rules for forty years.

**12th–13th century**
Rule of Zagwe dynasty; churches at Lalibela built.

**1270**
Yakuno Amlak reclaims throne for Solomonic line.

**1314–1344**
Reign of Amda Siyon; *gult* system established.

**1316**
Amda Siyon conquers Muslim community of Yifat, beginning long conflict with Muslims.

**1332**
Muslim holy war declared against Ethiopia.

**1434–1468**
Reign of Zara Yakob.

**1528**
Muslims take highlands after Battle of Shimbra Kure.

**1540–1559**
Rule of Emperor Galewedos; Muslims pushed out of high-lands.

**1541–42**
Lebna Dengel uses Portuguese assistance against Muslims.

**1563–1597**
Rule of Sarsa Dengel; strategic downsizing of empire.

**1607–1632**
Rule of Emperor Susenyos; his conversion to Roman Catholicism and attempt to force new religion on Ethiopia lead to his downfall.

**1632–1667**
Rule of Emperor Fasil; establishment of new capital at Gonder.

**mid-1700s–mid-1800s**
*Zamana Masafent* (The Age of the Princes).

**1855**
Tewodros II crowned, ending *Zamana Masafent* and uniting Ethiopia.

**1868**
Tewodros commits suicide; Yohannes IV becomes emperor.

**1876**
Menelik II becomes king of Shewa.

**1889**
Yohannes IV killed in battle; Menelik II becomes undisputed leader of all Ethiopia; Menelik II signs Treaty of Wechale.

**1895**
Italy invades Tigray; Battle of Adwa fought.

**1913**
Menelik II dies; Zauditu and Ras Tafari Makonen begin rivalry for power.

**1930**
Zauditu dies; Ras Tafari Makonen crowned Emperor Haile Selassie.

**1935**
Italy invades Ethiopia from base in Eritrea.

**1936**
Italian attack at Maychew; Haile Selassie flees Ethiopia, addresses League of Nations.

**1937**
Assasination attempt on Italian viceroy results in mass murder, arrests, and atrocities against Ethiopians.

**1941**
Combined British and Ethiopian forces push Italians out of Ethiopia.

**1973**
First in a series of droughts kills 250,000 in Tigray; Haile Selassie puts down peasant protests by force.

**1974**
Haile Selassie deposed; skeleton of Lucy found; first *Derg* leader, General Aman, killed by other committee members.

**1977**
Mengistu Haile Mariam's last rival, Tafari Bente, is killed; Mengistu becomes head of *Derg* and leader of Ethiopia.

**1991**
Mengistu escapes to exile in Zimbabwe.

**1995**
President Negasso Gidada and Prime Minister Meles Zenawi begin terms of office.

**2000**
National elections scheduled.

# Glossary

**Amharic:** The language of the Amhara people, still the main language used in government and business.

**arable:** A term used for land suitable for agriculture.

**cooperative:** a system of farming or industry where people pool their equipment, land, and supplies, work together, and share the profits.

*debtera:* A church musician and scholar of the arts.

**deforestation:** The cutting down of forests.

**desertification:** Loss of formerly arable land to poor land management or natural causes such as drought.

*Derg:* "Committee"; the name given to the ruling group after the fall of Haile Selassie.

**Falasha:** Ethiopian Jew.

**Ge'ez:** The language of the Aksumite empire, still used in scripture today.

*gult:* Land given by king as a reward for loyalty.

**pastoralist:** Living by following flocks; nomadic.

*ras:* "Head"; a term used for a noble.

*rist:* A landholding system where a whole family group, including future descendants, is perceived as having rights to a plot of land and cannot sell, give away, or otherwise lose it.

*shamma:* A shawl used to cover the shoulders, arms, and sometimes head.

**Solomonic:** Referring to rulers claiming to have descended from King Solomon.

**stela (pl. stelae):** A very tall, narrow single block of stone carved in the shape of a tower or obelisk.

**subsidy:** A price set far below the actual value as an incentive.

**subsistence farming:** Farming done to the extent necessary to meet the needs of a family rather than to produce crops for sale.

**teff:** The most common grain in Ethiopia.

**Tigrinya:** The language of the Tigray.

**villagization:** A term used during the *Derg* for efforts to move Ethiopians from tiny communities to villages with several hundred homes.

# SUGGESTIONS FOR FURTHER READING

## BOOKS

Daniel Abebe, *Ethiopia in Pictures*. Minneapolis: Lerner, 1988. Simple information and format but now a bit dated.

Dennis Brindell Fradin, *Enchantment of the World: Ethiopia*. Chicago: Childrens Press, 1988. Good general information but now a little dated.

Steven Gish, *Cultures of the World: Ethiopia*. New York: Marshall Cavendish, 1996. Recently updated volume with a great deal of good information about contemporary Ethiopia.

Jane Kurtz, *Ethiopia: The Roof of Africa*. New York: Dillon Press, 1991. Good basic text by an author who lived for years in Ethiopia.

Alan Moorehead, *The Blue Nile*. New York: Vintage Books, 1983. First published in 1962, this classic work traces the stories of four men who ruled or explored the region of the Blue Nile.

## WEBSITES

**Addis Tribune** (http://addistribune.ethiopiaonline.net). Online news service from Addis Ababa's main newspaper.

# WORKS CONSULTED

## BOOKS

Philip Briggs, *Guide to Ethiopia.* Old Saybrook, CT: Globe Pequot Press, 1998. One of the few guidebooks treating only Ethiopia rather than eastern Africa as a whole, this book is full of useful information for tourists as well as others interested in Ethiopian culture and history.

Simon Broughton et al., eds., *World Music: The Rough Guide.* London: Rough Guides, 1994. Excellent survey of musical styles and artists around the world, including a good section on Ethiopia.

Basil Davidson, *Africa: A History.* New York: Collier Books, 1991. Revised and expanded edition of a classic text by a noted scholar of African history.

*Ethiopia: A Country Study.* 3rd ed. Washington, DC: Library of Congress, 1993. One in a series of country studies by the research division of the Library of Congress, this volume contains extremely detailed information about the economy, government, and society of Ethiopia, although it is now in need of updating.

Donald N. Levine, *Greater Ethiopia: The Evolution of a Multiethnic Society.* Chicago: University of Chicago Press, 2000. A historical, sociological, and anthropological approach to understanding the uniqueness of Ethiopian society today.

Peter Manuel, *Popular Musics of the Non-Western World.* New York: Oxford University Press, 1988. Good, although somewhat technical discussion of non-western music, including information about Ethiopian popular music.

Harold G. Marcus, *A History of Ethiopia.* Berkeley: University of California Press, 1994. One of the few full-length histories exclusively of Ethiopia, acclaimed as the outstanding book in its field.

Kazuyoshi Nomachi, *Bless Ethiopia.* Tokyo: Odyssey Publications, 1998. A magnificent collection of photographs with accompanying text by renowned photographer Kazuyoshi Nomachi, including a preface by noted scholar and historian Richard Pankhurst.

*Post Report: Ethiopia.* Washington, DC: United States Department of State, 1996. A publication provided to government employees sent to Ethiopia, which supplies basic information about the country for those planning to live there.

John Reader, *Africa: A Biography of the Continent.* New York: Vintage Books, 1997. Excellent new history by a noted scholar.

Raymond A. Silverman, ed. *Ethiopia: Traditions of Creativity.* Seattle: University of Washington Press, 1999. Excellent book with many photographs, discussing in full chapters the various art and handicraft forms and the most prominent artists in Ethiopia today.

Julia Stewart, *Eccentric Graces: Eritrea and Ethiopia Through the Eyes of a Traveler.* Lawrenceville, NJ: Red Sea Press, 1999. A former Interaid International and United Nations World Food Program worker, Stewart relates her experiences traveling over extensive periods of time in Eritrea and Ethiopia.

## PERIODICALS

Angela Fisher, "Africa Adorned," *National Geographic,* November 1984.

Curt Stager, "Africa's Great Rift," *National Geographic,* May 1990.

## WEBSITES

**African News Online** (www.africanews.org). Articles from various news sources including the *Addis Tribune* and the Panafrican New Agency.

**AOL Ethiopia** (www.aol.ethiopia.com). Reprints of articles from Reuters news service.

**Ethiopian News Agency** (www.telecom.net). A source of articles about contemporary events in Ethiopia.

**Lonely Planet** (www.lonelyplanet.com). A good on-line source for travel and background information on Ethiopia.

**Mbendi** (www.mbendi.co.za). An African company focusing on corporations, management, and information systems involved with Ethiopia and other African nations.

**Netnation** (www.etonline.netnation.com). A host service of Netnation offered to assist small business in Africa.

**ReligiousTolerance.org** (www.religioustolerance.org). A site dedicated to researching and disseminating information about world religions and clarifying misperceptions that can lead to intolerance.

**Walta Information Center** (www.telecom.net). News articles focusing on world affairs, diplomacy, and other topics relating to politics and culture in Ethiopia.

# INDEX

# PICTURE CREDITS

# ABOUT THE AUTHOR

Laurel Corona lives in Lake Arrowhead, California, and teaches English and humanities at San Diego City College. She has a master's degree from the University of Chicago and a Ph.D. from the University of California at Davis.